Latitude Hooks
and
Azimuth Rings

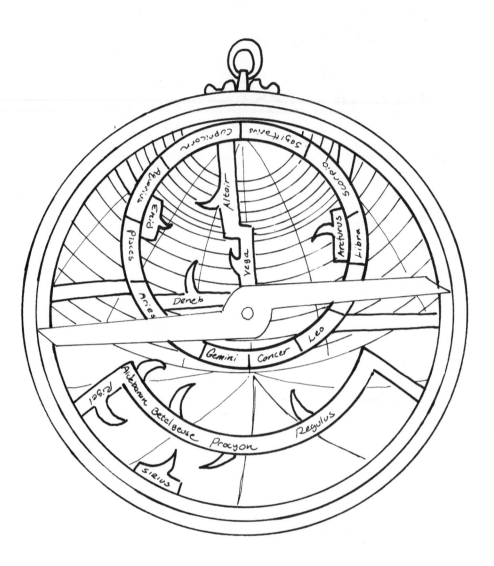

Latitude Hooks and Azimuth Rings

HOW TO BUILD AND USE 18 TRADITIONAL NAVIGATIONAL TOOLS

DENNIS FISHER

Illustrations by Joseph Fisher and the author

 INTERNATIONAL MARINE
CAMDEN, MAINE

To our parents,

and to Sue

❦

**International Marine/
Ragged Mountain Press**
A Division of The McGraw·Hill Companies

10 9 8 7 6

Copyright © 1995 International Marine, a division of The McGraw-Hill Companies.

Library of Congress Cataloging-in-Publication Data
    Fisher, Dennis.
       Latitude hooks and azimuth rings : how to build and use 18 traditional navigational tools / Dennis Fisher : illustrations by Joseph Fisher and the author.
          p.   cm.
       Includes bibliographical references (p. 161) and index.
       ISBN 0-07-021120-5
       1. Nautical instruments—Design and construction. 2. Navigation—Equipment and supplies—Design and construction I. Title.
    VK573.F56   1994
    623.8'63—dc20   94-37164
                                                                        CIP

Questions regarding the content of this book should be addressed to: International Marine, P.O. Box 220, Camden, ME 04843

Questions regarding the ordering of this book should be addressed to: The McGraw–Hill Companies, Customer Service Department, P.O. Box 547, Blacklick, OH 43004, Retail customers: 1-800-262-4729; Bookstores: 1-800-722-4726

Latitude Hooks and Azimuth Rings is printed on acid-free paper.

Printed by *Malloy Lithographing*
Design by *James Brisson*
Production and page layout by *Janet Robbins*
Edited by *James R. Babb, John Vigor*

Contents

Acknowledgments

T HANKS TO THE FOLLOWING for their help and support:

Our parents, Rose and Jerry Fisher; Susan Roberts; Nancy Noble and Kate Giordano of the Portsmouth Public Library; Robin Le Blanc; Doris Pailes; Professors R. Mark Benbow, Colin MacKay, and Michael Birkel of Colby College; Bobbie Ransley of the Portland Historical Society; Cindy Bendroth of the Rhode Island Historical Society; Rhode Island historian Doug Reynolds; Portsmouth naval historian Richard E. Winslow; N. Lyles Forbes, Assistant Curator of the Peabody Museum, Salem, Massachusetts; Jimmy White; and especially International Marine editors James R. Babb and John Vigor.

Thanks also for technical advice from boatbuilders Gordon Swift, Bob McLaughlin, and the late Bud McIntosh; Terry Pratt, Howard Moulton, H. Peter Barlow, Michael Urban, Phil Davis, and Bob Fish of the U.S. Coast Guard Auxiliary.

We are indebted to the works of Jean Randier, E. G. R. Taylor, Captain John Davis, Edmund Gunter, Bruce Bauer, Alan Villiers, and M. V. Brewington.

We would also like to thank the Mystic Seaport Museum; the New Bedford Whaling Museum; the Peabody Museum; the Maine Maritime Museum; the Portsmouth Atheneum; the British Museum, London; the National Museum of American History; the National Maritime Museum, Greenwich, England; the Baker Library at Dartmouth College; the New Hampshire State Library; and the Museum of the History of Sciences, Oxford, England.

Introduction

THIS BOOK IS FOR PEOPLE WHO LIKE TO WORK with their hands and who appreciate traditional nautical methods of navigation. You don't have to be the master of any craft to undertake any of these projects, just a careful and enthusiastic worker.

The projects fall roughly into three categories: decorative, useful, and somewhere in between. Some, such as the astrolabe, are mainly for display. On the other hand, the sounding line is an important and practical tool for small-craft navigation, particularly in the absence of an electronic sounder. The cross-staff falls somewhere in between, equally at home in the den or the ditch kit.

Each of the devices discussed here has, at one time or another, been used for the practical business of navigation, and each is worth reviving for its beauty, historic value, or sheer usefulness.

In designing the projects, I have emphasized simplicity and reasonable cost. Everything can be scratch-built from easily obtainable materials and tools. While few of these instruments are slavish copies, all are true to the spirit and function of the originals. They are not intended to be museum-grade reproductions of actual historic instruments. No two instruments were exactly the same in the days before industrialized mass production. So the ones you make will be every bit as authentic, and as individual, as the originals.

The history of navigation has always been the result of practical people making the best use of the means and materials at hand. As each generation of mariners sought to answer the question "Where am I?", the instruments in this book were invented, rediscovered, and redesigned in a diversity that defies the imagination. The astrolabe is reborn as the azimuth circle, the planisphere becomes the Rude star finder, and an ancient Polynesian tool is reinvented by a shipwrecked sailor to measure his drift across leagues of trackless ocean.

Nothing useful is lost completely. This is as true today as it ever was.

Tools and Materials

Y OU DON'T HAVE TO OWN or invest in lots of exotic tools to make the projects in this book. Most of the tools you'll need can already be found in any good home workshop or obtained through a tool catalog or lumberyard. The following list includes the tools you'll need to build all the projects in the book, but not every grade of sandpaper or weight of parchment paper is spelled out. Experienced wood and metal workers don't need such advice, and ordinary common sense will suffice for beginners still honing their skills. Incidentally, you don't need power tools for any of these projects, either. Nobody had power tools when the originals were built. But they'll save you a lot of time if you do have them.

However, to get the best results, your tools must be in good condition and you must know how to use them properly. Cutting tools, especially, need to be kept sharp and clean, and must be handled with care and prudence so they don't injure you.

Tools You'll Need

- ¼-inch mortising chisel
- Assorted wood and metal drill-bits
- Assorted craft wood knives
- Assorted straight-tip screwdrivers
- Bench vise
- Carpenter's square
- Carpenter's hammer
- Coping saw with wood cutting blades
- Files, single-cut, for finished work
- Files, double-cut, for rough work
- Flexible spines for drawing curves
- Fretsaw
- Hacksaw
- Hand brace
- Hand drill
- Handsaws—rip, crosscut, and tenon
- Metal clamps or weights
- Miter box
- Sliding bevel square
- Tape measure and yardstick
- Various grades of sandpaper and emery cloth
- Wood rasps (several sizes)

You will also need a pair of compasses, a pair of dividers, a protractor, and a ruler. Invest in good-quality instruments; you can always use them in your navigation kit, if you don't have them there already. A 360-degree protractor with a leg is also useful.

For lettering and other purposes, you'll need art brushes, a pen and India ink, or a permanent marker. Lines drawn with an artist's nibbed pen look much better than those drawn with a ball-point pen or felt-tipped marker. Calligraphic nibs will also improve the look of your letters and numbers. Spattering can be avoided with practice.

Tools It Would Be Nice to Have

Hand Tools

- Anvil, for hammering and bending metal pieces. I use a 1-foot section of railroad track.
- Hammers, wrenches, pliers, and wirecutters
- Various chisels, gouges, and hand-planes

Power tools

- ⅜-inch reversible electric drill
- Acetylene torch and equipment for brazing or silver soldering.
- Bandsaw
- Circular saw, such as a Skilsaw
- Drill press
- Router
- Sabersaw with carbide-coated blade
- Scroll saw
- Table saw with carbide-tipped blade
- Vibrating engraving tool
- Woodburning tool

Incidentally, miniature power tools, such as the Dremel Moto-tool, are good for cutting, grinding, carving, sanding, routing, buffing, polishing, engraving, and drilling. A basic machine costs about as much as a good electric drill.

Materials

All the materials you need can be found in hobby shops, art-supply shops, lumberyards, hardware stores, and in some cases, marine-supply stores. Most materials are inexpensive, especially in the small quantities you'll be using, but with careful craftsmanship they can be turned into instruments that will look and function like the original.

Wood

Lumberyards are a good source for most of the woods you need, and you can often find what you need in cheaper, leftover lengths. Where plywood is called for, use a good-quality, exterior-grade sheet with presentable veneers on both sides.

You can use fancier hardwood plywoods if you like, and if you can afford them. Marine plywoods command an exceptionally high price, and can be hard to find. However, you may be lucky enough to find a source of offcuts. But, except for the chip log (Chapter 15), marine ply isn't necessary.

Traditionally, nautical-instrument makers selected heavy, durable woods that didn't shrink or swell much. Ebony and rosewood were clear favorites because of their excellent dimensional stability, but some early wooden instruments were also made of fruitwoods such as apple or pear. Boxwood was preferred for the parts of an instrument to be engraved.

Ebony and rosewood are now rare and costly, although affordable in the small quantities you'll need. For a more reasonably priced alternative with a similar density, consider purpleheart. Mahogany is another good, all-purpose wood for nearly any application. Boxwood can still be found in hobby shops. And there are many other woods you could use, of course, including, in some instances, clear pine. Just trust your common sense.

Adhesives

While any number of adhesives can be used to build these instruments, I like epoxy because it's waterproof and can bond wood to wood, wood to metal, or metal to metal. Epoxy is even strong enough to make low-stress edge welds between metal sheets. Don't breathe the fumes, though. And wear plastic or latex gloves when handling epoxy.

Resorcinol glues are excellent for making tough, waterproof bonds between wood parts. For gluing paper to cardboard, use rubber cement. Glue both surfaces and allow them to dry before sticking them together. Yellow, aliphatic wood glues like Elmer's or Franklin Titebond are excellent adhesives but are not waterproof.

Finishes

The final finish you use is a matter of personal preference. Traditionally, instruments such as the octant, backstaff, and nocturnal were protected by rubbing in a hot polish made from melted beeswax and a little turpentine. You can make it yourself. Thin the wax with just enough turpentine to allow it to soak into the wood. The turpentine will evaporate and leave the wax in the grain. Any modern furniture polish containing beeswax in a soluble oil also is effective. You'll find several types in furniture stores and on supermarket shelves.

Though not traditional, a coat of yacht spar varnish is a fine way to finish most projects, or you can brush on an exterior polyurethane varnish or a stain-varnish combination. Wipe-on stains in the form of a paste are simple to apply and also do a good job, but may not be as durable.

You can also impart an antique look to wood by fumigating it with ammonia. Just enclose the instrument in an old trunk or a plastic bag with a cupful of ammonia for a few days and the wood will become noticeably darker.

Whenever you glue, paint, stain or varnish, first test your materials on scrap pieces to make sure they are compatible.

Metals

Any instrument used around the water should use hardware and fasteners of brass, bronze, or Monel metal, which is an alloy of nickel and copper. Brass will corrode badly in a salt atmosphere, but is suitable if it is protected by wood or a coating of paint or varnish. Bronze and Monel are very resistant to corrosion, although bronze eventually acquires a greenish-blue patina that many find attractive. All three metals are non-ferrous (an important consideration when a compass is nearby), and their soft luster does a great deal to impart an antique look to any device.

You'll find brass, bronze and Monel metal fasteners in most marine-supply stores or you can order them (as well as sheet brass and thin hardwood planks) from a good ship-modeling supply catalog such as Model Expo—see Appendix A. If you plan to build a piece for practice, or only for display, there's no harm in using cheaper, steel screws and nails, as long as they don't show and as long as you don't wave them around near a steering compass.

Most hobby shops sell sheet brass for a few dollars a linear foot. You can cut it with a sabersaw if you back it up with a piece of composite board to avoid distorting the metal. Remove burrs with a single-cut file. Remember always to put the piece you are working on in a clamp, preferably at waist height, and to chalk your file between uses to keep metal filings out of the teeth. Use draw filing to finish a piece and to remove any cross filing marks: Clamp the piece securely, hold the file at right angles to the work with both hands, and draw the file toward you. For a fine finish, wrap the file in emery cloth.

Hard soldering, either brazing or silver soldering, will join pieces of brass permanently. Soft soldering, using an alloy of tin and lead, is usually not strong enough.

Liver of sulfur (potassium sulfide) may be used as a coloring agent to make metals look older. Look for it in pharmacies and jewelry stores.

Shellac will help keep metal from tarnishing. Use a camel's hair brush and work in one direction only—never back and forth. Lacquer, in spray cans, is also available.

Face Material

Though engraved metal was a common feature in traditional nautical instruments, instrument makers began gluing printed paper faces to nocturnals, astrolabes, quadrants, and a number of other devices shortly after the advent of printing presses. This saved them from the laborious task of engraving the wood faces and helped make their instruments more affordable and widely available.

You can recreate these faces using papers, inks, paints, and brushes found in hobby or art stores. I prefer a parchment-type art paper that gives an antique look to display projects such as the backstaff arcs. However, you might want to ask an engraver listed in your Yellow Pages what it would cost to have such faces as the degree scale for the octant, and other faces, made in brass, or even silver. For some projects, prices are very reasonable. Some full-sized faces are provided in this book, ready to be photocopied.

You'll find many uses for carbon paper. With it, you can transfer patterns to wood or metal, or transfer lines and figures to the face of an instrument before inscribing or incising them.

Everything is Flexible

Nothing I have written in this book about any project is set in stone. The more advanced craftsperson who wants to embellish or elaborate on these plans should by all means do so. I also urge you to do your own research. Illustrations and descriptions of nautical paraphernalia abound and you may find something you like better than the plans I have provided. Besides, such research will certainly increase the personal value of your instrument.

CHAPTER 2 The Latitude Hook

T HE HISTORY OF THE PACIFIC PEOPLES is intimately connected with navigation and seamanship. And one of the most important navigational tools these explorers used was the latitude hook, a simple device made from split bamboo and twine.

Starting perhaps about in 800 AD, they began an eastward migration across the Pacific in fast, seaworthy sailing canoes. Eventually, they discovered and settled almost every inhabitable island in that vast ocean, including desolate Easter Island. They may even have reached the coast of South America.

When you consider that at the same time most European sailors still clung to the coastlines in slow, dumpy vessels that were little better than those of the Romans, the navigational achievements of the Pacific Islanders were quite astounding. Only the Vikings were making similarly daring voyages in their fast, narrow, longboats.

It's true that the islanders met by Cook and Bligh were ignorant of the compass, sextant, charts, and all the other navigational paraphernalia that made the voyages of *Endeavour* and *Bounty* possible. The navigators of the Pacific relied instead on their exceptionally keen observations of the stars and their environment, and on knowledge handed down from their forebears.

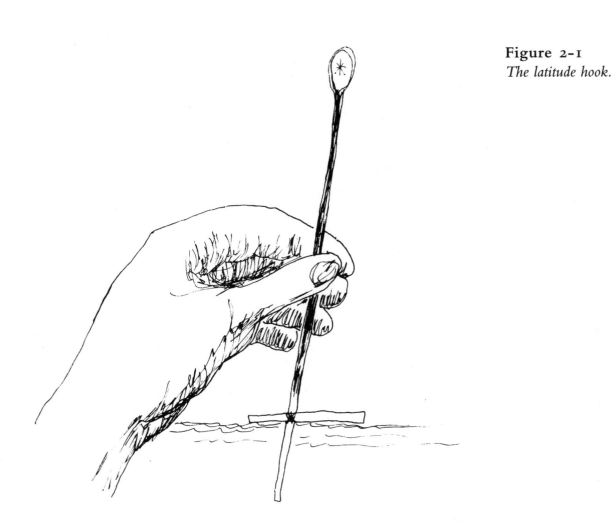

Figure 2-1
The latitude hook.

One of the few mechanical aids the Pacific Islanders did use was the Marshall Islands "chart." This cat's cradle of split bamboo and shells is actually a complex mnemonic device, or memory aid, showing the location of islands, currents, reefs, and the regular patterns of swells that occur around islands.

Another important device was the latitude hook, which consisted of a straight piece of split bamboo with a loop at the top, and another, shorter length of bamboo, known as the pointer, tied at right angles to the looped piece.

The hook relies on the fact that the stars appear to rotate around a fixed point known as the celestial pole. In the northern hemisphere, the north celestial pole is marked by Polaris, the North Star. At any time of night, it remains nearly at the same point in the sky. Its degree of altitude above the horizon always equals the latitude of the observer to within one degree, or 60 miles. For greater accuracy, a correction may be applied. This is described in Chapter 8.

What the latitude hook did was to measure the angle between

Figure 2-2
A Marshall Islands "chart."

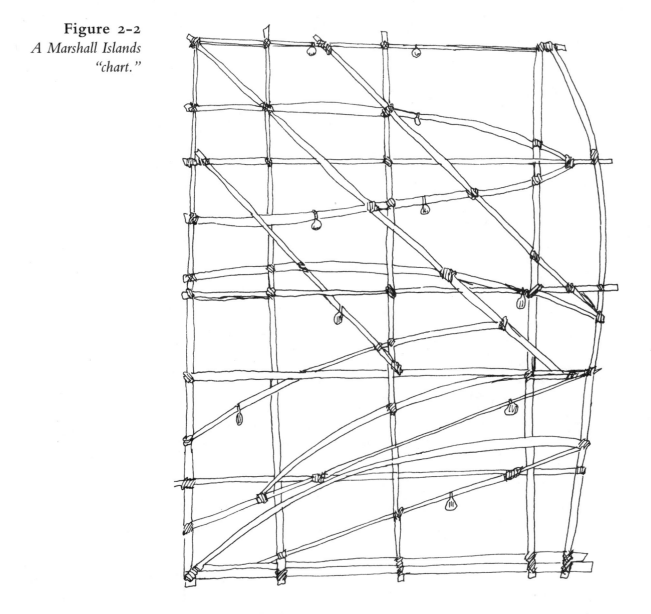

Polaris and the horizon. When it was held at arm's length and the pointer aligned with the horizon, a navigator knew he was maintaining his latitude if he could see Polaris through the loop.

If the star were above the loop, he would head farther south; below the loop, he'd head north. A Pacific navigator with a latitude

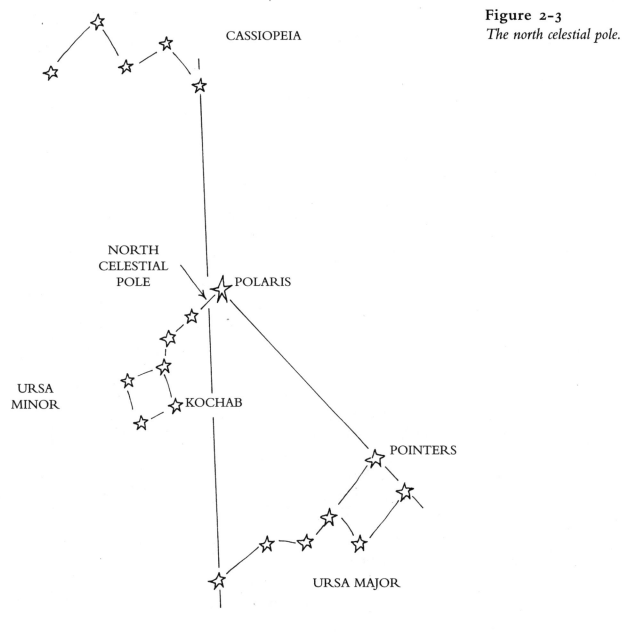

Figure 2-3
The north celestial pole.

CASSIOPEIA

NORTH
CELESTIAL
POLE

POLARIS

URSA
MINOR

KOCHAB

POINTERS

URSA MAJOR

Figure 2-4
The south celestial pole.

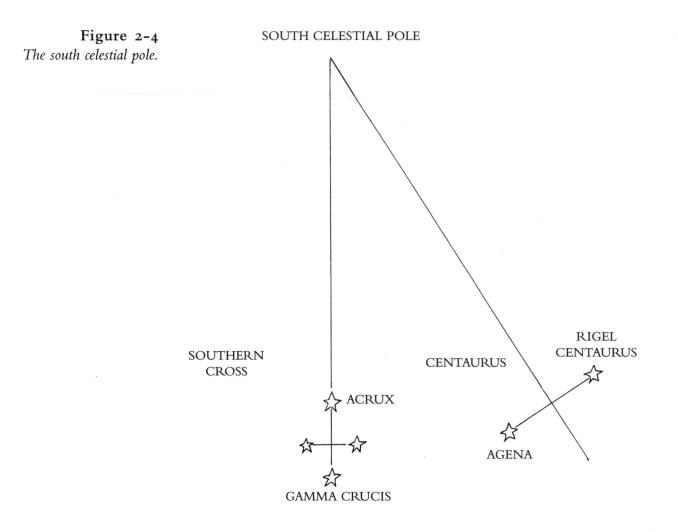

SOUTH CELESTIAL POLE

SOUTHERN
CROSS

CENTAURUS

RIGEL
CENTAURUS

ACRUX

AGENA

GAMMA CRUCIS

hook could find his way to any island on the same latitude as the one he'd left. Islands at higher or lower latitudes required hooks of different lengths.

In the South Pacific, in latitudes where Polaris is not visible, islanders may have sighted the south celestial pole through their latitude hooks. Because the southern pole has no marker star like Polaris, they had to intersect two imaginary lines sighted from the constellations Southern Cross and Centaurus.

They also had another, cruder method of finding the southern pole. That was to use the two stars that point directly at it. These pointers are the stars that form the long axis of the Southern Cross. The distance to the pole is five times the distance between the pointers, which may be estimated reasonably accurately.

While easy to use and fairly foolproof, latitude hooks are prone to errors from ocular parallax, a distortion caused by the user's trying to look in two directions at once—toward the horizon and toward the star.

Another error creeps in when the user of a latitude hook accidentally varies the distance between the hook and his eye. It must be held at the same fixed distance for every measurement, usually at arm's length. But moving a shoulder forward or back can alter that length.

As an aid to dead reckoning, however, the hook is still useful and fun to use aboard any modern pleasure craft, and for emergency navigation it could be a lifesaver, even though it gives only an approximate indication of latitude. Indeed, it has proved its utility to at least one modern-day navigator.

Steve Callahan, who spent 76 days in a rubber liferaft after his small sloop sank on a transatlantic passage, devised something like a cross between a latitude hook and a cross-staff to keep track of his position. Callahan lashed three pencils together to form a triangle, then sighted along one pencil to the horizon and along another to Polaris. The angle formed by these two pencils, which he measured by laying his instrument on the compass rose of his chart, indicated his rough latitude.

His sights weren't off more than a degree or two over 1,800 miles. As each degree of latitude equals 60 nautical miles, his position was accurate to within 120 miles or so. Such accuracy, gained from three pencils lashed together, is remarkable, though doubtless it was due more to his skill as a navigator than to the quality of his instrument.

The value to Callahan of knowing his position cannot be overestimated. Not only did it boost his morale, it helped him calculate the location and timing of his landfall and determine the best time to use his Emergency Position Indicating Radio Beacon (EPIRB) to improve his chances of rescue.

Using Your Latitude Hook

Let's presume you have made a latitude hook for your present latitude. On a fine night, when Polaris is easily visible, hold the shaft vertical, using the horizon pointer to help you keep it upright, and aim toward the star.

With the bottom of the horizon pointer just kissing the horizon, Polaris should appear smack in the middle of the loop.

If you are not on your latitude, and wish to regain it, you must head south if Polaris is above your loop, and north if Polaris lies below it.

The authors of the American Practical Navigator, *often referred to as* Bowditch, *note that a ruler held at arm's length, with your thumb at the horizon and the top end at the star, may also be used to find latitude.*

For instance, if Polaris appears 10 inches above your thumb and the distance from your eye to the ruler is 23 inches, you can draw a simple right-angle triangle with a base 23 units long and a perpendicular side 10 units high—any convenient unit will do. If inches become too unwieldy, try centimeters, or use your dividers.

Then simply measure with a protractor the angle formed between the base and the side opposite the right angle.

That's your latitude.

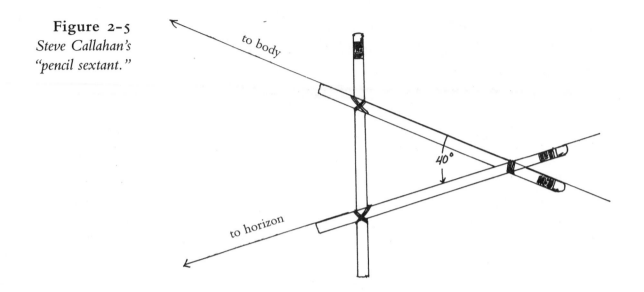

Figure 2-5
Steve Callahan's "pencil sextant."

to body

40°

to horizon

Making a Latitude Hook

Here's what you'll need:

- Two bamboo skewers, ⅛" × 12", OR
- One hardwood dowel, ¼" × 24"
- Thread
- Wood glue

To build a latitude hook of the sort used by the Pacific Islanders, take a 12-inch bamboo kebab skewer about ⅛-inch in diameter and cut off its sharp end. Now take another skewer and cut off a piece 2½ inches long. From what remains of this second skewer, shave off a thin, 2-inch-long strip with an X-Acto knife, then boil the shaving in water until it is flexible enough to bend. About one minute of boiling is sufficient.

Remove the strip from the water with a slotted spoon and form a loop no more than ⅜ of an inch in diameter. Fix the loop in place with thread on one end of the longer bamboo piece, and let it dry. When it is dry, and its shape is permanently set, remove and discard the thread. Glue the loop in place, secured with fresh thread, and rub a little glue over the thread to strengthen it, if you like.

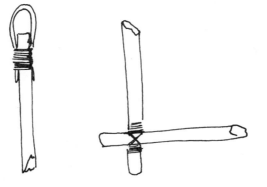

Figure 2-6
Construction details: the loop and the horizon pointer.

Now hold the hook at arm's length so Polaris can be seen through the loop sight and carefully note where the hook's shaft crosses the horizon. Glue and tie the 2½-inch pointer here. Your latitude hook is finished.

A 12-inch skewer is long enough only for use in latitudes up to 30 degrees north or south. You can find the exact length of a latitude hook for higher latitudes by drawing a right triangle on a large sheet of paper, with the bottom side equal to the distance from your eye to your hand and the bottom acute angle equal to the latitude required.

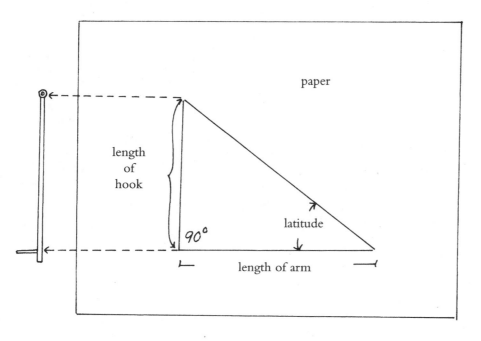

Figure 2-7
Drawing a right triangle to find the correct length of a latitude hook.

Figure 2-8
*Using a ruler as a
latitude hook.*

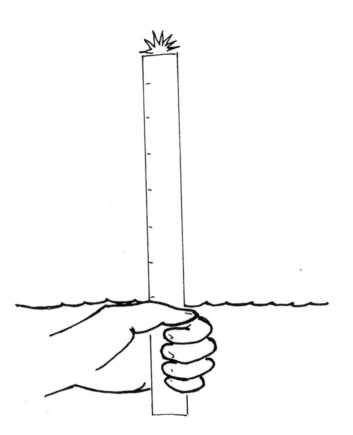

The length of the side opposite this angle will be the loop-to-pointer length.

Longer latitude hooks can be fashioned from a piece of stiff wire. Just make a loop at one end and bend the other at a right angle where it crosses the horizon.

Likewise, a ¼-inch wooden dowel with an eyescrew or bamboo loop on one end and notches cut for various latitudes will also serve. Adding a string, with a knot held in your teeth, or a wooden arm, will keep your hook the same distance from your eye every time you take a sight and will make your measurements more precise.

The Kamal

Arab mariners were navigating the Indian Ocean long before Sinbad sailed on his quasi-mythical voyages at the end of the first millennium. When Vasco da Gama rounded the Cape of Good Hope five hundred years later, he found the descendants of Sinbad in great merchant dhows plying the long trade routes along the perimeter of the Indian Ocean. They still do, to this day.

From the Strait of Hormuz at the mouth of the Gulf, dhows would venture east through the Gulf of Oman, past Ras al Hadd at the entrance to the Arabian Sea, before heading south across the Gulf of Aden to Cape Guardafui on the Horn of Africa. Running down the coast, a dhow might trade at Mogadishu, Lamu, and Mombasa before returning home with the new monsoon, perhaps loaded with mangrove logs cut from coastal swamps, or with a cargo of ivory, slaves, and spices for a trading run to India.

To accomplish such formidable voyages, dhow captains relied for navigational help on an astoundingly simple device of wood and string called a *kamal*, or guide. Of course, they also had local information and knowledge handed down from their fathers, who were almost always dhow captains too. Sailing instructions were also included in chart books that illustrated the geography of different coasts. And a dhow

Figure 3-1
The kamal.

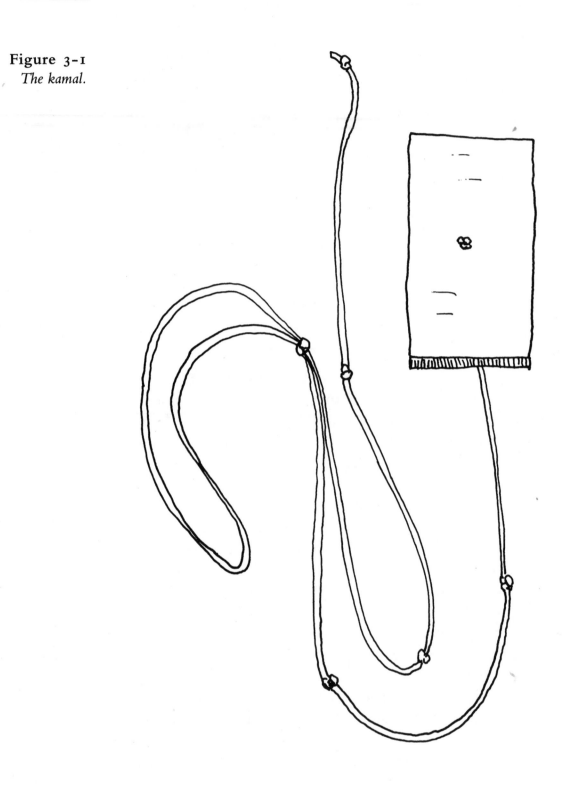

might have a compass, though the quality of these instruments varied considerably.

But it was the kamal that guided them safely across vast stretches of the Indian Ocean. This simple tool enabled them to find a specified latitude. Once they reached the correct latitude, they simply had to run due east or due west to find port.

The kamal is surprisingly efficient at measuring relatively small angles, and thus is of most use in the lower latitudes near the equator. It consisted of a small board with a hole drilled in the center and a knotted string that passed through the hole. The knots in the string corresponded with the latitudes of certain key ports and waypoints.

While the kamal worked on the same principle as a latitude hook (Chapter 2), its knotted string represented a major advance over the Pacific Islanders' tool. The string kept the board a fixed distance from the eye, which allowed more accurate sightings, provided an exact record of important waypoints, and enabled one instrument to be used over a wide range of latitudes. Practically speaking, the kamal enabled a *nakhoda*, or dhow captain, to stay safely out at sea—away from dangerous, often pirate-infested, coastal waters—and still remain reasonably sure of his position.

Figure 3-2
Arab navigator using a kamal.

Using Your Kamal

Using the kamal is simple. On a night when you can see the North Star, take the string in your mouth and position the knot for your destination latitude against the back of the kamal board.

Hold the board out with your left hand so that its bottom edge is aligned with the horizon and the string is taut. With your right hand, pull the opposite end of the string down so the knot won't slip through the hole.

If the North Star touches the top edge of the kamal board, you know you have reached the same latitude as your destination. All you have to do now is run due east or west.

If the star lies above the kamal, you must head south.

If it lies below, head north. Don't be afraid to experiment with your kamal. Many people find it more practical to tie the knots in the mouth end of the string, with a large stopper knot behind the hole through the kamal. Then you can use the instrument with one hand and use the other to steady yourself.

A kamal also can be used upright, and calibrated to read degrees of arc. Some sailors using a kamal this way drill two holes through the kamal in a vertical line, near the edges, and rig a small bridle ending in a single string to the mouth. That helps keep the kamal vertical when

(continued on page 21)

Making a Kamal

Here's what you need:

- One piece of fine wood such as teak, oak, or mahogany, 3" × 1¾" × ¼"
- Mason's twine, 8 feet

Drill a hole in the center of the board slightly larger than an overhand knot tied in the string, then sand and finish it. You might want to stain the wood or fumigate it with ammonia to simulate age.

Hold the string in the middle, so the ends hang down. Two feet below the middle, knot the string together to form a loop. This is the mouth knot that is held between the teeth when taking a sight, thereby keeping the kamal board a fixed distance from the eye while the sight is taken.

The best way to determine where the board knots should be tied is to sight the North Star, Polaris, from the latitude you wish to find again. With one end of the string held tightly in your mouth, slide the kamal outwards until its bottom edge rests on the horizon and its top edge just touches the star. Tie an overhand knot loosely at the board end. Holding the end of the string downwards at a right angle with your free hand prevents it from running back through the hole.

Now test the position of the knot again. The kamal, with its long edge kissing the horizon, should exactly fill the space between the horizon and the North Star. If it doesn't, make small adjustments to the knot until it is accurate. Then tighten the knot.

If you would like to set up the knots in advance, for the latitudes of ports you're going to visit, you'll need to construct a diagram like Figure 9-4 on page 71.

Hold the mouth knot at the centerpoint of the protractor, slide the board along the string until it touches the appropriate latitude marking, then tie a knot in the string on the side of the board opposite the mouth knot. Once all the knots are tied, slip one end of the twine through the hole in the board and tie a stopper knot, such as a figure eight, so board and string won't ever be separated.

Because dhows ranged great distances north and south, a kamal might have two boards, one larger than the other, to locate Polaris in the higher and lower latitudes. Your 3-inch × 1¾-inch board will serve for the lower latitudes, up to 20 degrees; a 6-inch × 3½-inch board attached to the other length of string exiting the mouth knot will work in the higher latitudes, up to 40 degrees. To get an idea of how large a board needs to be for your particular latitude, refer to the Latitude-Crosspiece table on page 70. The crosspiece length will correspond to the height of your board. Follow the same procedure described above to tie the mouth knots for the larger boards.

You can record what each knot means on the back of the boards. You might also want to add a phrase in Arabic, such as the universal dhow sailor's blessing: "Allah karim"—"God will help."

you're sighting, which is important.

The kamal is very reliable at reproducing measurements of small angles and it is unusually versatile. If you calibrate it, you can use it to find your distance offshore, for example, or from an island of known length. You can use it, if you have a chronometer, to find the time of Local Apparent Noon, which gives you your longitude. And this humble piece of wood and string can even double as a sun compass.

CHAPTER 4 The Astrolabe

THE ASTROLABE IS AN ANCIENT ASTRONOMICAL and surveying instrument for finding the altitude of celestial bodies, and the heights of buildings or mountains. It was probably invented by the Greeks. Its name means, literally, "star-taker." Basically, it is a disk marked off in degrees of arc around its circumference, with sight vanes on a rotating pointer called an *alidade*. The disk, which is usually made of brass, hangs vertically from a ring by which the astrolabe is held above the viewer's head.

A navigator or astronomer would turn the alidade until the star or planet could be seen in a straight line through both the pinhole sights, or pinnules, in the sight vanes. The angle of this line above the horizon, as indicated by the alidade, can be converted into latitude.

On land-bound instruments, sightings read down from the zenith, at 0 degrees, and are known as zenith distances. When these are subtracted from 90 degrees, you get the altitude of the body above the horizon. If Polaris is the body being sighted, its altitude above the horizon is your latitude, uncorrected for seasonal variations. For practical reasons, sailors later reversed the degree scale so that 0 degrees represented the horizon and 90 degrees was straight overhead.

The astrolabe was the first of the versatile scientific instruments

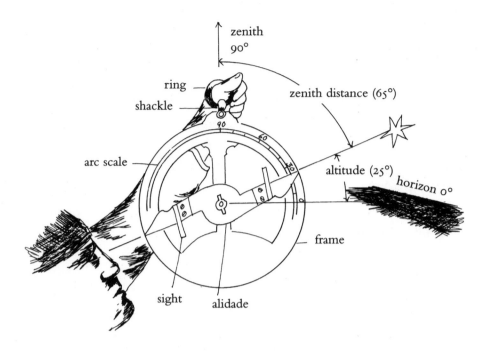

zenith
90°

ring
shackle
zenith distance (65°)

arc scale

altitude (25°)
horizon 0°

frame

sight   alidade

Figure 4-1
The mariner's astrolabe.

used by navigators. Unlike the latitude hook or kamal, discussed in Chapters 2 and 3, it can be adapted to many situations and functions.

With an astrolabe, for instance, you can also find a celestial object's azimuth, its relative bearing from true north. Lay the astrolabe flat with 0 degrees pointing north and aim the alidade at the point on the hori-

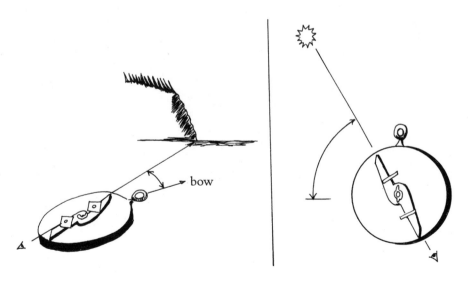

bow

Figure 4-2
Taking a relative bearing (left) and finding the sun's altitude (right) with the astrolabe.

zon directly below the star. The azimuth can then be read from the degree scale. This is a key piece of information for celestial navigators seeking to establish lines of position.

The Arabs refined the astrolabe into a highly artistic and multipurpose device. Their elegant instruments had a planisphere on the reverse side made up of an ornamental fretwork plate called a *rete*, engraved with the names of important stars. Each star had a fixed pointer marking its relative position on the celestial sphere. The rete turned on a *mater*, a removable holding plate inscribed with elliptical lines showing declination and azimuthal coordinates.

Figure 4-3
The rete and the mater.

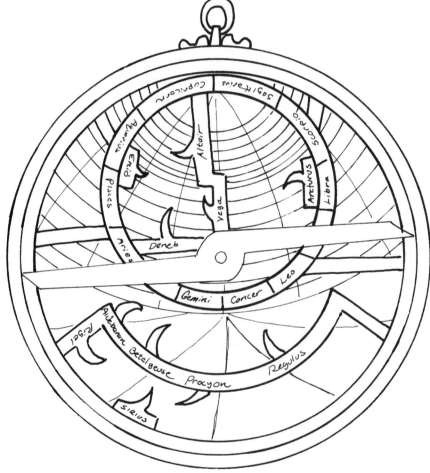

Different plates were inserted at every other degree of latitude and the rete was rotated to the day and hour of observation so that the navigator would know where to look for key stars. The principle is similar to that used by the Rude star finder, which helps modern celestial navigators find the best stars for observation on any night and at any latitude. In a sense, the planisphere was an early analog computer for tracking the motions of celestial bodies.

Arab camel drovers crossing the great deserts of Arabia and Africa were probably the first to navigate with astrolabes. They found their latitude by noon sights—adding or subtracting the sun's declination (its angular height above the celestial equator) to or from its zenith distance, depending on the season—or by sighting on Polaris.

By the 15th century, mariners had adopted the astrolabe for use in ocean navigation. One change they made was to engrave two mirror-image arcs on the upper hemisphere of their astrolabes, both having 90 degrees at the zenith and 0 degrees at the horizon. This innovation allowed the instrument to be used with equal facility by right- and left-handed navigators. It also allowed mariners to read altitude directly from the scale, instead of having to subtract the zenith distance from 90 degrees.

But taking accurate sights with an astrolabe, a relatively simple proposition in a flat, stable desert, was next to impossible aboard a ship at sea. Usually three men were required. One braced his back against the mainmast while holding the instrument aloft. Another sighted the star. The third would read the angular height from the degree scale. Lining up the dimly shining Polaris through pinhole sights on a pitching, rolling deck demanded more skill than most seamen had, and if a breeze caught the instrument, sight taking was nearly impossible.

To overcome the effects of wind and the ship's motion, marine astrolabes were often as small as 6 or 7 inches in diameter, and as heavy as 4 pounds. An astrolabe, however, is accurate in direct proportion to its size; a large instrument shows minute and second gradations more clearly than does a small one. As a result, errors of up to 5 degrees were common on the smaller marine instruments.

The Portuguese explorer Vasco da Gama circumvented these problems by going ashore to take sights with a large, wooden astrolabe hung from a tree branch. But for mariners far out at sea, the astrolabe was of limited use. Columbus had an astrolabe on his first voyage, but apparently never got accurate readings from it.

Despite the astrolabe's limited accuracy, it continued to be used in improving forms until well into the 18th century. Unlike the cross-staff, backstaff, and octant (Chapters 9, 10, and 19), the astrolabe needs no horizon. Gravity does the work of aligning the instrument so star sights can be taken on the darkest nights. An astrolabe can also be used as a pelorus (Chapter 17) for taking relative bearings or as a handy aid for finding stars. Besides, the beauty and elegance of this device make it a fine object for display.

While even the simplest brass astrolabe requires metal-machining and engraving skills beyond the scope of this book, handsome wooden models can be built in any workshop. Two versions are offered here: a solid-frame astrolabe like the kind used for astronomy, and a mariner's astrolabe with an open-fretwork frame to minimize windage.

Making an Astronomical Astrolabe with Paper Face

Here's what you'll need:

- One hardwood or plywood board, ½" × 8" × 8" (if you can't find hardwood this wide, edge-glue two pieces together)
- One hardwood board or piece of plywood, ¼" × 5 ½" × ½"
  One piece .025" sheet brass, ⅞" x 3"
- One brass ring, 1½"diameter
- One brass bolt(³⁄₁₆" × 1") with brass wingnut and three brass washers
- One bronze shackle with ¼"-diameter pin
- Four small brass screws
- Drawing paper
- Sandpaper
- Stain and varnish
- Epoxy glue

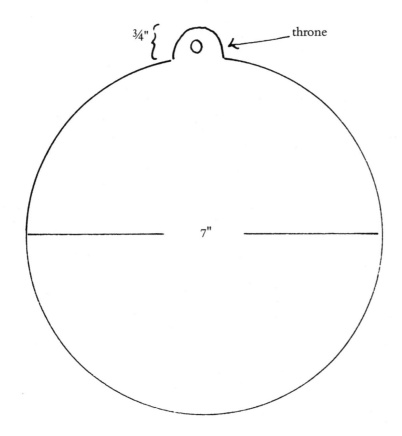

Figure 4-4
The disk with throne.

To make the disk, use a pair of compasses to draw a 7-inch circle on the hardwood or plywood board. Cut it out with a sabersaw or bandsaw, making sure to leave a ¾-inch × ¾-inch *throne* at the top (Figure 4-4) to accommodate the ring handle.

With the compass on the same centerpoint, lightly scribe a 6-inch circle on the disk. Then drill a ⁵⁄₁₆-inch hole through the centerpoint, the exact center of the disk. Also, drill a ⁵⁄₁₆-inch hole in the throne, as shown in Figure 4-4. Sand and finish the disk with stain or varnish, then draw a light pencil line connecting the center of the throne hole with the hole at the center of the disk.

For the paper face, take a compass and a piece of drawing paper and scribe a 6-inch diameter circle. Then transfer the markings from a protractor to the degree scales, as shown in Figure 4-5. You can decorate the face as shown, use zodiacal symbols, or draw a simple star map from any astronomical text. Cut out the finished face and glue it to the

THE ASTROLABE   **27**

wooden disk with a light application of a white glue such as Elmer's Glue-All. Use the 6-inch circle you drew on the base to position the paper, and line up the 0-degree mark on the outside of the face with the pencil line connecting the throne hole with the disk's center hole. Once in place, erase the pencil line and protect the paper with several coats of shellac.

Make the alidade from the ¼-inch stock using a scroll saw or sabersaw, and carefully drill a ³⁄₁₆-inch pivot hole at the alidade's exact center using a drill press. If the pivot hole is not centered, your astrolabe will not be accurate. Sand and finish the alidade with stain and varnish.

Figure 4-5
Sample paper face.

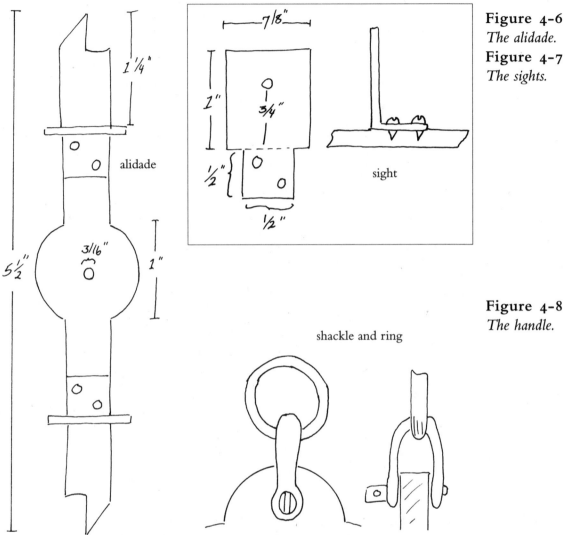

Figure 4-6 *(left)*
The alidade.
Figure 4-7 *(right)*
The sights.

Figure 4-8
The handle.

To make the two sights, cut the sheet brass with a hacksaw, following the pattern in Figure 4-7. Then clamp the sights together so the edges line up, mark the metal with a scratch awl ¼ inch from the top edge and ⅞₆ inch from the side edge. At that mark, drill an ⅛-inch sight hole through the mark and through both sheets.

Bend the sights into right angles, and secure them to the alidade, 1¼ inches from the tips, using epoxy glue and small brass screws so their pinnules are exactly in line with the pivot hole—see Figure 4-6. Brush-on shellac, or spray-on lacquer, will protect the metal from tarnishing.

A simple bronze shackle, available from any marine hardware store or marine catalog, serves to join the throne to the brass ring. Secure it so the astrolabe hangs freely. It is important that the shackle not bind against the throne.

Attach the alidade to the disk with the brass bolt, washers, and wingnut. When tightened, the wingnut holds the alidade in place after a sight is taken.

Making a Mariner's Astrolabe

Here's what you'll need:

- One piece hardwood or plywood, ⅜" × 11" × 11" (If you can't find hardwood this wide, edge-glue two pieces together.)
- One piece hardwood, ¼" × 2" by 10"
- One piece .032" sheet brass, 2" × 5"
- One brass ring, 1½" diameter
- One brass bolt, ³⁄₁₆" × 1¼", with brass wingnut and three brass washers
- One bronze shackle with ¼"-diameter pin
- Drawing paper
- Stain and varnish
- Sandpaper
- Epoxy glue or brass screws

The steps for constructing and assembling the mariner's astrolabe are essentially the same as for the astronomical astrolabe. First, cut the 10-inch disk and throne from the 11-inch-square board. Then, using carbon paper, transfer the scaled-up design from Figure 4-9 to the board and cut out the fretwork with a sabersaw or scroll saw. Drill a ³⁄₁₆-inch center hole and a ⁵⁄₁₆-inch shackle-pin hole, then sand and stain the frame.

Using Your Astrolabe

By eye, estimate the altitude of the star or planet you want to sight, and set the alidade for this figure. Now, with your thumb through the ring, hold the astrolabe so that the pivot of the disk, the star, and your eye are all in line. Rotate the alidade until you see the star through both sights. Now, gently tighten the wingnut, lower the instrument, and read the arc.

You can take sun-sights, too, but since looking directly into the sun is painful and damaging to the eyes, it's safer to take sun sights by holding the astrolabe near the ground. Move the alidade until the sun shows directly through the sights and focuses one pinpoint of light on the ground. Then tighten the wingnut as before, and take your reading.

If you know the latitude of
(continued on page 31)

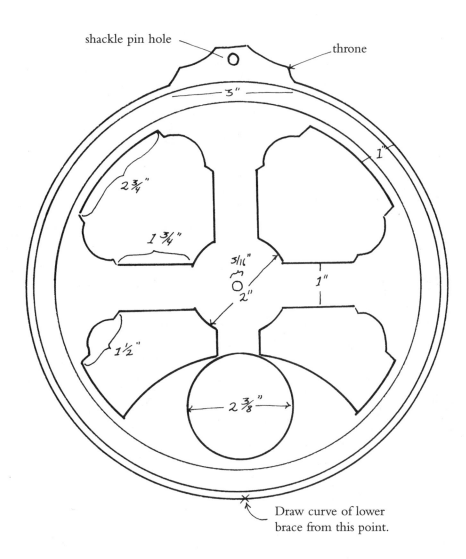

shackle pin hole

throne

3"

1"

2 3/4 "

1 3/4 "

3/16"

2"

1"

1 1/2 "

2 3/8 "

Draw curve of lower
brace from this point.

Figure 4-9
*Astrolabe construction
details.*

*your location, you can determine
the accuracy of your instrument
with simple sight of Polaris,
taken on land. The altitude of
Polaris above the horizon should
correspond with your known latitude. But don't expect too
much. If you get closer than 1
degree (60 nautical miles) you're
doing pretty well.*

*Your astrolabe also will give
you the horizontal angle between
two prominent landmarks on
shore, which makes it a valuable
instrument for coastal navigation.
Simply turn it on its side and
point the baseline (0 degrees) at
one object. Then move the alidade until the second object lines
up through your sight holes.
Gently tighten the wingnut and
read the angle. Combined with a
magnetic bearing on one of the
objects, this will give you a posi-
tive position fix.*

You can photocopy the full-sized paper scale onto parchment
paper and glue it to the disk with Elmer's Glue-All, or you can inscribe
the various lines shown directly on the wood with pen and ink or an
engraving tool. If you choose the latter method, transfer the scale to the
wood with carbon paper. Whichever way you choose, make sure the
90-degree mark on the scale lands on a line connecting the center of
the shackle-pin hole and the center hole on the disk. When you're finished, protect your handiwork with several coats of varnish.

Figure 4-10
Degree scale.

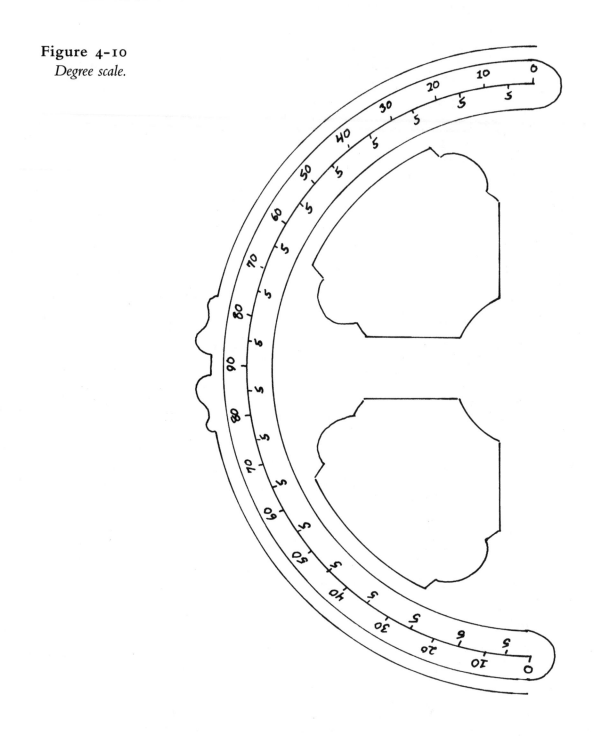

LATITUDE HOOKS AND AZIMUTH RINGS

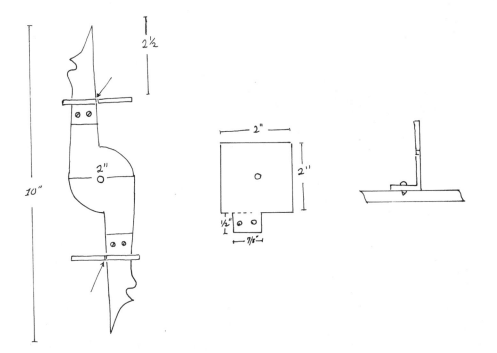

Figure 4-11
The alidade and sights.

Cut the alidade out of your ¼-inch stock using a scroll saw. As before, drill both sights at the same time, then bend and fasten them to the alidade with small brass screws and epoxy glue so that the pinnules line up with the center of the pivot hole.

The handle of this instrument consists of a ring and shackle, as in the astronomical astrolabe (Figure 4-8).

5 The Quadrant

T HE QUADRANT, LIKE THE ASTROLABE (Chapter 4), is an astronomical instrument that mariners adapted for use at sea. The name quadrant comes from the quarter-circle encompassed by its arc, and in its simplest form the quadrant is nothing more than a 90-degree protractor with a plumb bob or plummet hanging from its apex.

Astronomers made extensive use of the quadrant. It was well known to the Arabs. Tycho Brahe, the 16th-century Danish astronomer, used a room-sized version to make his stellar chart, from which Johannes Kepler eventually made his great discoveries. Columbus had one, though he had as little success with it as he had with the astrolabe. He complained in his log about not being able to use his instruments except in a virtual flat calm, and even then his measurements were off by as much as 19 degrees.

As a dead reckoner and rhumb-line navigator, Columbus mostly wasn't bothered about finding his latitude at sea. He did, however, use his quadrant to find the latitude of Jamaica.

Instead of a degree scale, the early quadrants used by sailors had the names of important ports written in appropriate places along the arc. When the cord cut the arc at a place name, the navigator knew it was time to start running east or west along that line of latitude to the

Figure 5-1
Working with the quadrant—from an ancient woodcut.

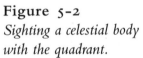

Figure 5-2
Sighting a celestial body with the quadrant.

destination. In this way, quadrants were similar in usage to the Arab merchant's kamal (Chapter 3).

It took two persons to sight with a quadrant aboard ship—one held the instrument and sighted on the body, the other read the altitude from the arc. In heavy weather, this operation was almost impossible to perform accurately, even if the star in question could be easily seen.

As with the astrolabe, the larger the quadrant, the greater the accuracy. There is a limit, of course, to the size of instrument that could be handled and stowed aboard ship. The instructions here are for a 10-inch version.

In theory, gravity-aligned devices like the quadrant and astrolabe can be used at any time of day or night, and are not, like the sextant (Chapter 19), limited for star sights to twilight hours or moonlit nights when the horizon also is in view. In practice, however, a star or planet has to be quite bright to be seen through the sights of these instruments. Polaris is a fairly dim star, hard to sight from the heaving deck of a ship.

Though the quadrant's ability to accurately determine latitude at sea leaves much to be desired, it is easy to use and never needs adjustment. It is practically indestructible, floats, and can be employed both for celestial navigation and for pilotage. As we saw with Steve Callahan's adjustable latitude hook (Chapter 2), such simple navigational devices can be invaluable in a pinch.

Making a Quadrant

Here's what you'll need:

- One hardwood, plywood, or pine board, ½" × 10" × 10"
- Two pieces .025" or .032" sheet brass, ½" × 2"
- One round-head brass screw, ¾" long
- Four small brass screws
- Heavy-duty carpet thread, 15" length

- One ¼" bead with hole same size as string
- Plumb bob, lead sinker, or monkey's fist
- Drawing paper
- Pen and ink
- Paint, or stain and varnish

The quadrant's frame is made from the 10-inch square board. Using a pair of compasses, draw an arc with an apex 1¼ inches from the top left corner (along the diagonal to the bottom right corner) and a radius of 9 inches. Cut along this arc with a sabersaw. Sand and finish with paint or stain and varnish, unless you plan to engrave or ink the degree scale directly onto the wood.

To make the degree scale, lightly scribe another pencil arc from the apex, which, as you'll recall, is 1½ inches in from the top left corner, along the diagonal. This time, make the radius 8 inches.

Now tape a piece of drawing paper over the work and draw the scale shown in Figure 5-3 with an ink pen and compass. The outer edge of the arc has a radius of 8 inches, like the one you just drew on the face of the quadrant. The next arc in has a radius of 7⅝ inches, and the innermost one a radius of 7¼ inches. Use a one-arm protractor to mark degrees as shown in Figure 5-3.

Cut out the scale and glue it in place with white glue, using the arc on the frame as your guide. Before the glue dries, take the one-arm protractor and make sure that the scale is positioned accurately. A line drawn through the apex, parallel to the left edge, should run exactly through 0 degrees. A line through the apex parallel to the top edge should run exactly through the 90-degree marking. Protect the paper with one or two coats of shellac.

If you choose, you can also transfer the scale to the board with carbon paper and then inscribe it on the wood with pen and ink or engrave it with a woodburning tool. Apply two or three coats of a clear finish to protect your handiwork.

To be accurate, a quadrant's sight holes must be precisely parallel with the quadrant top. The following steps will ensure your sights are a matched pair. First, lay the pieces of brass one on top of the other so

Figure 5-3
Construction details of the quadrant.

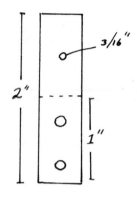

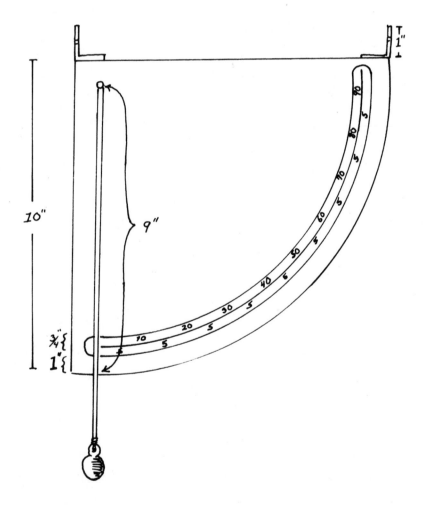

their edges line up, clamp them together, then drill a $\frac{3}{16}$-inch hole through both sheets. These will be the sight holes. Also drill two holes through both sheets for the screws that fasten it to the frame.

Next, unclamp the pieces, lay them side by side—edges aligned—and temporarily secure them to your workbench with a screw through their screwholes. Lay a steel rule across the middle of both sheets and scratch a line perpendicular to their length across both faces, using the rule as a guide and a awl or nail to make the scratch.

With a vise, bend each sight into an exact right angle at the scratch line. Check the right angle with a square. Now all that remains is to screw and glue the sights to either end of the top edge of the quadrant.

At the apex, drill a pilot hole for the brass screw (don't go all the way through the wood), put a drop of glue in the hole, and screw it in place. Leave $\frac{1}{4}$ inch of the screw's shank showing.

The string holding the plummet has to be strong but thin, since too thick a line will obscure the reading. Traditionally, silk cord was used.

Thread on the bead, which should be a fairly tight fit. Then tie one end of the 15-inch thread to the screw and the other to the plummet. The plummet can be any suitable weight—a lead sinker, a piece of brass, or a plumb bob. For a nautical look, use a monkey's fist (Chapter 14) tied around a stainless-steel ball bearing.

Making a Nunes Scale

Early seafarers dressed up their quadrants with innovations that improved the instrument's usefulness and versatility. One was the Nunes scale, invented by the Portuguese geographer and mathematician Pedro Nunes. The Nunes scale turned the quadrant into a simple analog computer or nomogram that showed the length of a degree of longitude at any parallel. This was (and still is) vital information for navigators.

A Nunes scale consists of a scale divided into 100ths and a semicircle that graphically represents the ratio of leagues to degrees of longitude at different latitudes.

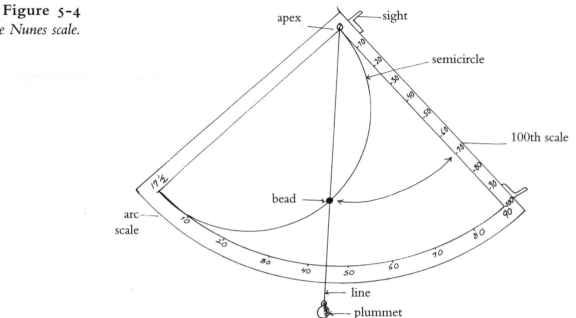

Figure 5-4
Details of the Nunes scale.

(Incidentally, the league is a confusing measurement that varied from 2½ to 4½ statute miles, depending on the country in which it was used. In English-speaking countries, it was three miles—statute miles on land and nautical miles at sea. But in this example, Nunes' league works out to about 3.43 nautical miles.)

In the semicircle's upper corner, at the quadrant's apex, is the number of leagues in one degree of longitude at 90 degrees latitude (0). At the bottom corner, the semicircle touches 17½ degrees, the number of (Nunes) leagues in one degree of longitude at the equator.

If you wished to moderize the scale you could, instead of 17½ degrees, make that figure 60, which represents the number of nautical miles in one degree of longitude at the equator.

The 100ths scale is constructed by dividing the distance between the apex and the arc scale into ten equal segments. The radius of the semicircle is exactly half the length of the 100ths scale.

Making a Geometrical Square

A second innovation adapted to the quadrant was a pair of numbered, diagonal scales known as a geometrical square. This square gave navigators a rough idea of the tangents and cotangents of the angles being measured. Tangents and cotangents enable a sailor to discover the height of any feature at a known distance, and the distance to any landmark of known height.

To make a geometrical square for your quadrant, place marks along the quadrant's straight edges that are 3 inches, 3¼ inches, 3½ inches, and 4 inches from the apex—see Figure 5-5. Now draw a perpendicular line from each mark to the middle of the quadrant (at the 45-degree line) to form four "half-squares." After placing a mark every ¼ inch along the perimeter of the third half-square from the apex, put a ruler at the apex and draw radial lines between the first and third half-squares at every third mark.

Between the second and third half-squares, draw a radial line from the apex at every mark—a total of 12 marks—then ink in every other

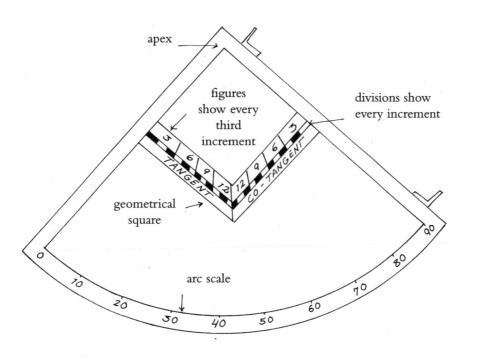

Figure 5-5
Details of the geometrical square.

To use a quadrant single-handedly, simply sight the celestial body through the peepholes and pinch the cord against the arc as soon as the sight is taken. Then, without shifting or letting go of the cord, bring down the instrument and read the altitude on the scale. That's where the cord cuts the arc. If you're sighting Polaris, the reading shows your rough latitude. A carefully made quadrant should be able to fix latitude within a degree or two, under the right conditions.

Like the astrolabe, the quadrant can be used to shoot the sun without looking directly at it. Just hold it close to the ground and align the sights so a single pinpoint of sunlight hits the ground.

rectangle to make the divisions easier to read. As a reminder, write "cotangent" in the space between the third and fourth half-square on the right side and write "tangent" in the corresponding space on the left side.

You can draw the Nunes scale and the geometrical square on parchment paper and glue them to the face with Elmer's, or use carbon paper to transfer your drawing to the wood, then engrave the lines and figures.

Using the Nunes scale

The scale is simple to use—see Figure 5-4. The cord is held at the degree of latitude in question, in this case 45 degrees, and the bead on the cord is moved up until it touches the semicircle. Without changing its position on the string and keeping the string tight, swing the bead to the right-hand scale. The number on this scale (70) is divided by 100 and multiplied by $17\frac{1}{2}$ to yield the number of leagues in a degree of longitude. At the 45th parallel, one must travel 12.25 leagues east or west to traverse one degree of longitude.

What the scale actually gives you, of course, is a percentage of a distance. In the example above, for instance, at latitude 45 degrees, the length of a degree of longtitude is only 70 percent of what it is at the equator, where it equals the degree of latitude—as far as practical mariners are concerned.

Thus, if you have modernized your Nunes scale to read 60 (nautical miles) instead of $17\frac{1}{2}$ (Nunes leagues), you'll find that a degree of longitude at 45 degrees latitude is about 70 percent of 60 miles, or roughly 42 miles.

Using the geometrical square

Sight the object through the peepholes. For angles less than 45 degrees, the cord cuts through numbers that approximate the tangents of the angles. Figure 5-6 shows that at 25 degrees, for instance, the cord cuts the scale at the number five. The tangent of this angle is approximately the ratio five to twelve.

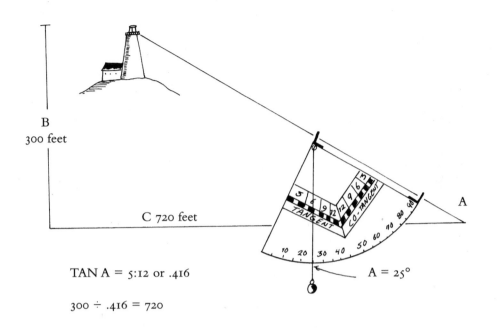

Figure 5-6
*Using a geometrical square
to find the distance to a
known height.*

B
300 feet

C 720 feet

TAN A = 5:12 or .416

A = 25°

300 ÷ .416 = 720

For angles greater than 45 degrees, the cotangent can be found on the adjacent scale. At 70 degrees, for example, the cord cuts the square at four, for a cotangent of around twelve to four.

Using simple trigonometry, the tangents and cotangents told the ancient navigator the distance he was away from a known height, or the height of an object if he knew his distance away.

We have come a long way since those times. The modern navigator who wishes to know how far away he or she is from a charted object simply measures its height in degrees and minutes and consults the conveniently pre-calculated Distance-Off Tables found in every standard reference work.

6 The Astronomical Ring

THIS INTRIGUING LITTLE DEVICE for determining the altitude of the sun is simply a circle hung from a ring. As in the astrolabe (Chapter 4), gravity aligns the ring with the zenith. A small hole in the ring, called a *pinnule*, allows a spot of sunlight to shine onto a graduated scale on the ring's inner surface. This shows the sun's altitude, from which latitude can be calculated.

Though not as accurate as an astrolabe, the astronomical ring is uncomplicated and easy to use. It helped mariners determine when the sun had reached its highest altitude, which made more accurate noon sights possible with the astrolabe.

Astronomical rings can be made from brass or from some resilient wood like ash that is steamed and bent into shape.

Making a Seven-Inch Astronomical Ring

Here's what you'll need:

- Wood strip, $\frac{1}{16}$" × 1" × 24", preferably ash or other straight-grained hardwood OR .025" brass sheet, 1" × 22"

Figure 6-1
The astronomical ring.

- ■ .025" brass sheet, 2" × 2"
- ■ Brass ring, 1½" outside diameter
- ■ Two brass bolts, ⅛" × ½", with nuts and washers OR two copper clench nails or split rivets, ½" long
- ■ Drawing paper

Making the Brass Ring

First, drill two ⅛-inch bolt holes ⅜ inch from the edge of the 22-inch brass strip and ¾ inch from each end as shown in Figure 6-2. Then drill an ⅛-inch pinnule sight in the center of the strip, 2¾ inches from one end.

To make the handle, cut out the 2-inch-square brass sheet following the pattern and dimensions shown in Figure 6-2 and drill two ⅛-inch bolt holes as shown. Now bend the handle's upper flange 90 degrees to the handle's base. Then wrap the flange around the 1½-inch brass ring. The handle's base must be cambered slightly to match the

Figure 6-2
Construction details for the brass astronomical ring.

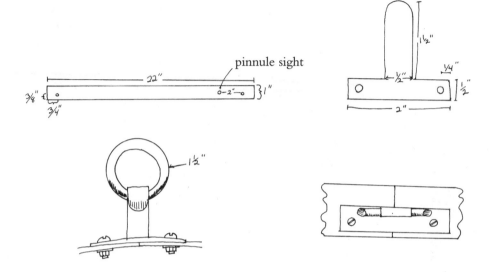

pinnule sight

*Using Your
Astronomical Ring*
*To find your latitude from a
noon sight, you need to take the
sight when the sun is at its
absolute zenith. But that rarely
coincides with noon on the clock.
So the only way to find the time
of local noon, if you don't know
your exact longitude, is to chase
the sun up to its zenith.*
*The sun rises all morning, of
course, but its arc seems to flatten
toward local noon, and it will
hang at the top of its arc for a
minute or two before beginning its
afternoon descent. Watching for the
pause at the zenith was far easier
with an astronomical ring because
the spot of light gave a visual
indication of the sun's highest altitude. It was then that the astrolabe
was called into use to take the*
(continued on page 47)

curve of the ring. Otherwise, the ring may deform when the handle is bolted on. You can bend the base around a metal pipe.

Finally, bend the 22-inch strip into a ring and fasten the handle in place with bolts or rivets. To ensure that your astronomical ring forms a perfect circle, make a wooden jig 1 inch thick and 7 inches in diameter and wrap the strip around it.

Making the wooden ring

First make the wooden jig mentioned above. Then taper the ends of the wood strip so they will form a 2-inch scarf joint when overlapped—see Figure 6-4. Then drill an ⅛-inch pinnule hole in the center of the strip 3¾ inches from one end. Steam or boil the wood until flexible, quickly bend it into a loop, and clamp it in place, with the tapers overlapping, around the jig.

Incidentally, steaming times will vary depending on the kind of wood you use. Test for flexibility after 10 minutes, and every 10 minutes thereafter. You can make a simple steamer out of a 2-foot-long piece of 1½-inch metal pipe and a teapot or saucepan. Stuff a porous rag in the top end, if necessary. Take care to protect your hands from the hot wood.

Figure 6-3
A simple steaming box.

Once the wood has cooled and dried, remove the clamp, glue the joint with epoxy or wood glue and clench the two copper nails against a metal pipe as shown in Figure 6-4. Fashion the handle out of sheet brass and attach it to the ring, as described above.

Making the Scale

Once the ring is made, the next step is to create the scale. Begin by cutting a strip of drawing paper 19 inches long by 1 inch wide. Tape it to the inside of the ring.

Now, take a compass, a protractor, and a piece of paper and draw a quadrant with a radius of 7 inches. Use a protractor to mark out the degrees within the quadrant. These degree markings must be long enough to intersect the ring; 2½-inch-long marks are sufficient.

Before you can transfer these marks to the ring, you need to find its vertical axis. You can do this by hanging the ring and a plumb line from a horizontal dowel. The plumb line should hang freely from the center of the dowel. Slide the plumb line next to the ring and mark

actual noon sight, which it could render far more accurately than the ring.

To take a sight with an astronomical ring, hold the ring by the handle so that it hangs freely. Face the pinnule sight toward the sun and observe where the sun strikes the scale. This is its altitude.

To convert this figure to latitude is a simple matter if you know the declination of the sun for the time of your sight. This information is given in nautical almanacs, published yearly. They are available at all marine stores.

For more information on working out a noon sight, see the sidebar in Chapter 19, "Using Your Octant." But don't expect your astronomical ring to be anywhere near as accurate as the octant.

Figure 6-4
Joint for wooden astronomical ring.

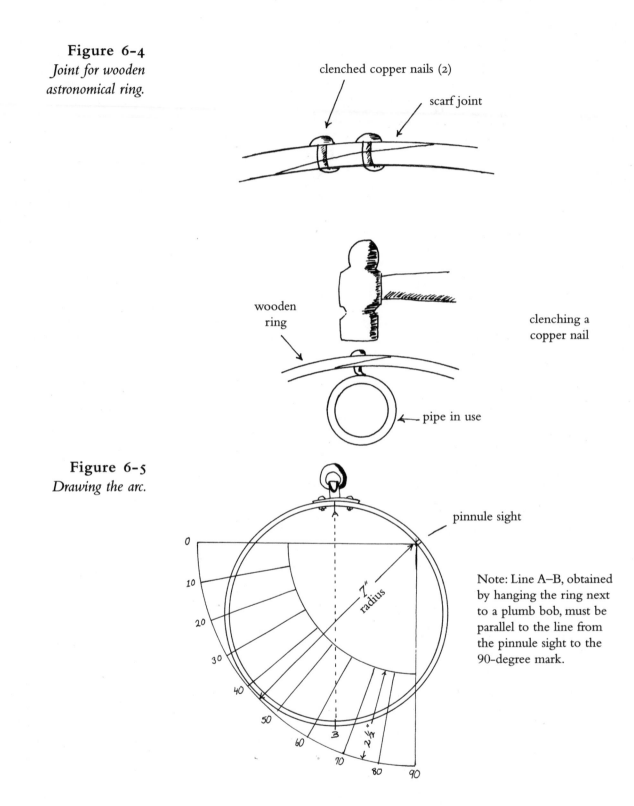

clenched copper nails (2)

scarf joint

wooden ring

clenching a copper nail

pipe in use

Figure 6-5
Drawing the arc.

pinnule sight

0
10
20
30
40
50
60
70
80
90

7" radius

3

2½"

Note: Line A–B, obtained by hanging the ring next to a plumb bob, must be parallel to the line from the pinnule sight to the 90-degree mark.

where the line touches the top and bottom of the ring. These two points are on the ring's vertical axis.

Lay the ring over the drawing of the quadrant so that the apex of the quadrant aligns with the pinnule sight, and so that the vertical axis of the diagram and the ring are parallel. Then carefully transfer the degree markings from the diagram to the ring's paper scale with a pencil. Once all the degrees are marked, make a pair of pencil marks across the paper's edge to the ring. These will serve as register marks so you can glue the scale in place accurately.

Now remove the scale from the ring, and ink in the degree markings and figures with a pen. After the ink is dry, glue the scale in place making sure you align the register marks. Use Elmer's Glue-All for the wood ring, epoxy for the brass ring. When the glue is dry, erase the register marks and protect the entire ring with two or three coats of shellac.

7 The Sundial

U<small>NTIL THE ADVENT OF THE CHRONOMETER</small> in the late 1700s, sundials and the half-hour sandglass were used for the timing of watches (sailors' duty times) and celestial observations. They also were used to calculate the ship's speed. Later, when clocks were in common use aboard ships, sundials were used as a rough check of the clocks' accuracy.

Sundials came in a many configurations: equatorial, vertical, pillar, diptych, cube, and armillary sphere. Here are two interesting types you can make—a horizontal sundial for use on shore, and a portable universal ring dial for use at sea.

Making a Horizontal Sundial

Here's what you'll need:

- Seasoned hardwood (mahogany or teak), ½" × 9" × 9"
- .032" sheet brass (or thicker), 8" × 8"
- Two roundhead brass screws, ½" long
- Two flathead brass screws, 1½" long
- One 4" × 4" post (cedar or pressure-treated), 5 feet long

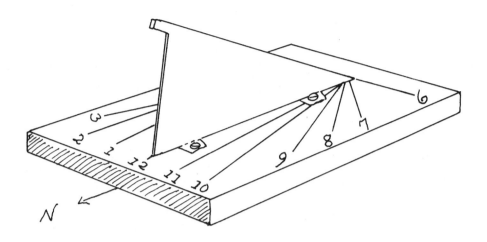

Figure 7-1
A horizontal sundial.

The horizontal dial has limited use at sea because to work it has to be level. But many fine examples can be found at sea captains' homes all over the world. Horizontal sundials have been made of all kinds of material, including ivory, brass, marble, wood, papier-mâché, bronze, jade, gold, silver, copper, and iron.

I use a stable, weatherproof wood such as mahogany or teak for the base and make the gnomon, or pointer, out of brass.

A sundial's base can be any size or shape. I chose 9 inches by 9 inches as a handy size for a backyard dial. Sand the face and lightly pencil in the hour lines and Roman numerals shown in Figure 7-2, using a ruler as a guide. Carefully paint the lines and figures with gloss black exterior paint.

A 4-inch × 4-inch post, set perfectly plumb in a sunny spot in your yard, makes a fine pedestal for a sundial. Make sure the sundial's base will be level when mounted on the post.

Drill and countersink two ³⁄₁₆-inch holes two inches apart on the base's 12 o'clock line, then temporarily fasten the base to the pedestal with one flathead screw. Use a non-ferrous screw so it won't affect the magnetic compass you'll use to align this centerline along the north-south axis so that 12 o'clock points to true north.

Remember that the compass itself doesn't point to true north, so you'll have to add or subtract your local variation. You can find the exact variation for your area, in degrees and minutes, on a nautical chart or a

Figure 7-2
Horizontal sundial face.

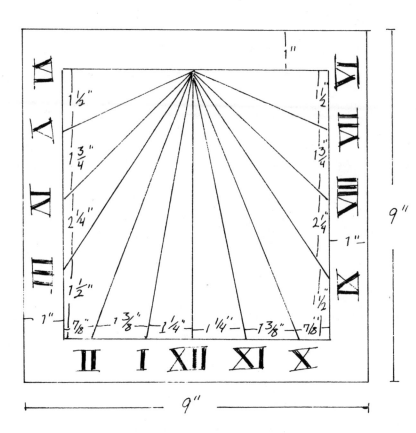

Figure 7-3
Aligning the gnomon.

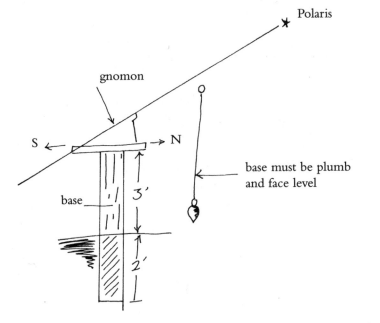

U.S. Coast and Geodetic Survey (USCGS) map. Round it off to the nearest degree.

Incidentally, these instructions apply for anyone in the northern hemisphere. If you live in the southern hemisphere, instructions regarding north and south should be reversed.

Once the base is properly aligned, carefully drive the second flathead screw through the base and into the post.

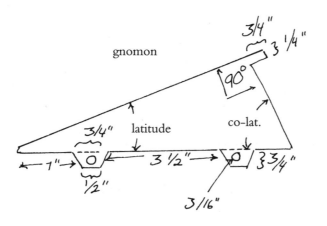

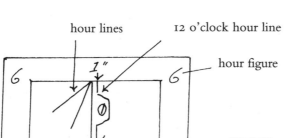

Figure 7-4
The gnomon—construction details.

top

Using Your Sundial

Even after the sundial is leveled and aligned, the shadow will not be totally accurate on most days. This is because the sun, as we see it, does not move at a uniform speed. Solar time therefore differs from the mean, or average, time we keep on our clocks by as much as 15 minutes, depending on the season. Readings from the sundial must therefore be corrected with an equation of time.

A graph of the equation of time (Figure 7-5) shows how many minutes to subtract from or add to the time shown on the sundial. On the first day of January, for instance, 5 minutes should be added to solar time to get clock time. By the middle of the month, 10 minutes need to be added. Note that on only four days of the year does sun time coincide with clock time—in early April, late May, in August and in December.

For the sundial to tell time reliably, the gnomon—the triangular, upright plate that casts the shadow—must be vertical, lined up along the true north-south axis. You can use Polaris to check it. See Figure 7-3.

The gnomon's south-pointing angle, the acute angle touching the base, must equal your local latitude. This compensates for the different slant of the sun's rays at different parallels.

The gnomon's top angle, the highest one off the ground, is always a right angle. It follows, therefore, that the final angle, the north-pointing angle at the base, must equal 90 degrees minus your latitude—which is the colatitude.

To avoid any errors when cutting the metal for the gnomon, draw a full-sized pattern on paper, then use carbon paper to transfer the pattern to the brass sheet. Cut the brass with a hacksaw or coping saw fitted with a metalworking blade.

The two tabs on the gnomon secure it to the sundial's base. Drill ³⁄₁₆-inch screwholes in the tabs and bend them 90 degrees. Now position the gnomon along the 12-o'clock line, centered ⅜ inch from each edge, and fasten it to the base with the ½-inch roundhead screws and epoxy.

The accuracy of your sundial depends on the gnomon's being exactly perpendicular to the base. Check the angle with a square. To ensure the base is aligned correctly, sight along the top edge of the gnomon. It should be pointing directly at the North Star—see Figure 7-3.

Figure 7-5
Equation of time, showing number of minutes to be added to, or subtracted from, sundial time to find mean (clock) time.

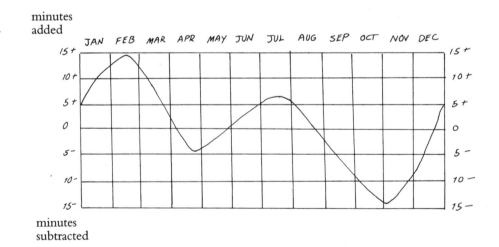

LATITUDE HOOKS AND AZIMUTH RINGS

Protect the wood with several coats of oil or varnish, and recoat once or twice a year.

Making a Universal Ring Dial

If you want a true, seagoing sundial, you can build a universal ring dial.

This unusual sundial, which can show the time at any latitude and season, is one of the few sundials that can be used with any accuracy at sea. Since it is held by a cord and leveled by its own weight—much like an astrolabe (Chapter 4)—it is not affected by a moderate swell and with

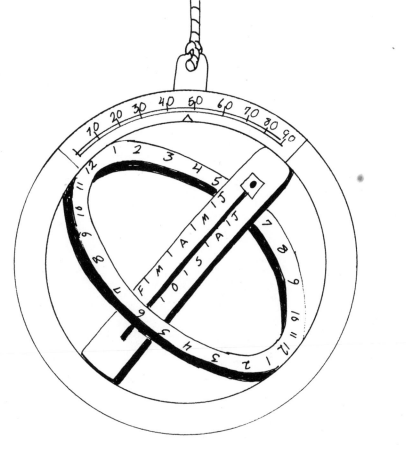

Figure 7-6
A universal ring sundial.

Figure 7-7
*Rings and gnomon—con-
struction details.*

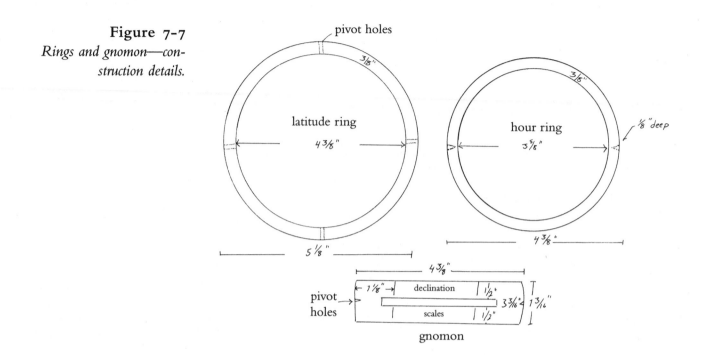

Figure 7-8
Faces for the sundial rings.

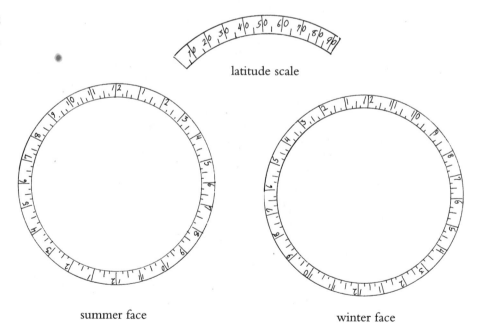

latitude scale

summer face

winter face

LATITUDE HOOKS AND AZIMUTH RINGS

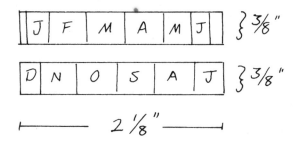

Figure 7-9
Declination scales for the gnomon.

care can be read while a ship is underway. The entire dial can be folded nearly flat for storage.

The dial consists of two rings and a bar. The outside ring is known as the latitude ring. Inside it is a pivoting hour ring. And through the middle, pivoting on the inside edges of the latitude ring, is a bar-shaped gnomon. This gnomon has a slot for a sliding pinnule that adjusts for the daily declination of the sun.

My ring dial is made of wood and metal, though an experienced metalworker could fashion one out of solid brass.

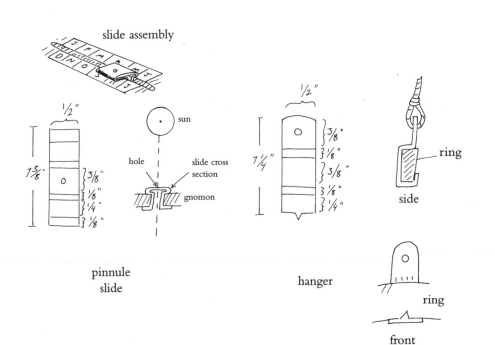

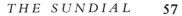

Figure 7-10
Details of pinnule slide and hanger.

Using Your
Seagoing Sundial

*Before using the sundial, turn
the hour ring so it is perpendicular
to the latitude ring with the clock-
wise-reading summer face up. Now
set the hanger's pointer on your latitude. Next, align the pinnule
alongside the date on the gnomon's
declination scale. This declination
scale reads monthly, from left-to-
right above the gnomon slot and
from right-to-left below the slot. For
example, January 1 is the left side
of the leftmost box above the gnomon's slot. July 1 is the right side
of the rightmost box below the slot.
Now consult your compass and
(making allowance for local magnetic variation) turn the sundial so
the upper end of the gnomon (the
end anchored at the 90-degree
mark on the latitude ring) points
to true north.
What you have here, in effect, is
(continued on page 59)*

Here's what you need:

- One piece hardwood or hardwood ply, ¼" × 4" × 4"
- Four brass brads, ½" long
- One sheet of parchment paper
- Two sheets .005" brass, 1⅜" × ½"
- Cotton string, 12"

First, draw the rings on the ¼-inch stock with a compass and cut out the pieces with a coping saw or scroll saw. If you cut carefully, you can use part of the inner section of the large ring for the gnomon. Make the gnomon and slot as shown, then sand and stain these pieces.

Now drill four pivot holes through the edge of the latitude ring, each 90 degrees from the other, and two ⅛-inch-deep pivot holes into the edge of the hour ring, each 180 degrees from the other. Also, make a ⅛-inch-deep pivot hole in the center of either end of the gnomon. You can use a brad as a drill bit to make these holes.

Take parchment paper, compass, and a small, one-arm protractor

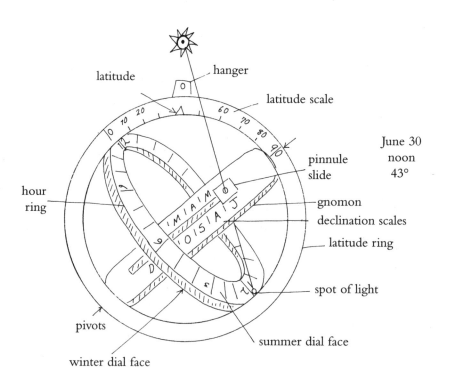

Figure 7-11
The ring sundial in action.

and draw the latitude scale and the two dial faces—a summer face with hour markings arranged in the normal clockwise manner, and a winter face that is its mirror image. The hour lines on the dial faces are 15 degrees apart.

Glue the hour faces to either side of the hour ring so they match up exactly and so the 12 o'clock marks line up with the ring's pivot holes. Likewise, glue the latitude scale to the face of the latitude ring so the 0-degree and 90-degree marks line up with the ring's pivot holes.

The declination scales in Figure 7-9 are full-sized, so you can copy them on a light table. Center and mount them on the gnomon with Elmer's Glue-All.

The hanger and pinnule slide are made from .005-inch sheet brass, which is light enough to cut with a pair of scissors and bend with needle-nosed pliers or your fingers. Follow the patterns in Figure 7-10.

The pinnule hole should be about $\frac{1}{32}$-inch in diameter; punch it out with a small nail. Bend and fold the slide as shown; its arms hold it in place while allowing it to move along the gnomon's slot.

Now bend the hanger around the latitude ring as shown so it fits tightly but can still be adjusted. Tie a length of cotton string to the hanger's hole.

To assemble the dial, insert the brads through the latitude ring's pivot holes into the appropriate piece. The hour ring pivots on its brads at the 0-degree mark on the latitude scale; the number 12 on the hour ring should be next to that 0-degree mark. The gnomon turns on the brads at, and opposite to, the latitude scale's 90-degree mark. See Figure 7-11.

a miniature representation of the earth, with the hour ring as the equator and the gnomon, as the earth's axis of rotation, pointing to the North Star.

Now rotate the gnomon so a pinpoint of sunlight passes through the pinnule and falls on the hour face. This shows the time of day. At noon, the shadow of the latitude ring, rather than a spot of sun, will mark the time.

To read the sundial in the summer (April to September), you'll need to look down on the dial to see where the sun hits the upper summer face. In the winter (October to March) when the pinnule slide has to be moved along the gnomon, hold the sundial aloft so you can see the spot of sun on the lower winter face. As with a stationary sundial, apply the equation of time (Figure 7-5) to convert solar time to clock time.

8 The Nocturnal

T HE NOCTURNAL IS A SOPHISTICATED VERSION of the earlier star clock. It tells time by tracking the position of stars in the two Bears (Ursa Major and Ursa Minor) or, in some nocturnals, Cassiopeia. Probably developed sometime in the 1200s and used by both Europeans and Arabs, the nocturnal has a sight, a pointer, and date and hour disks. They were often made of brass and could be quite elaborate. Seagoing nocturnals were commonly built of boxwood because it is a good medium for engraving.

In the years before astronomy and astrology permanently parted company, many nocturnals were engraved with zodiacal symbols and served astrological functions as well. Often, at the center of the face, there was a perpetual calendar indicating the phases of the moon, lengths of days and nights, holidays, sunrises and sunsets, and positions of the sun relative to the zodiac. Eventually, the nocturnal became an essential tool in the navigator's kit—a tool used for telling time, correcting latitude, and, by the mid-1700s, calculating tides.

Clocks were a rarity at sea long after they became common on land because the weight-driven types were not practical for sea use, and the spring-driven types were notoriously inaccurate. The humble and ancient nocturnal actually kept better track of time than the

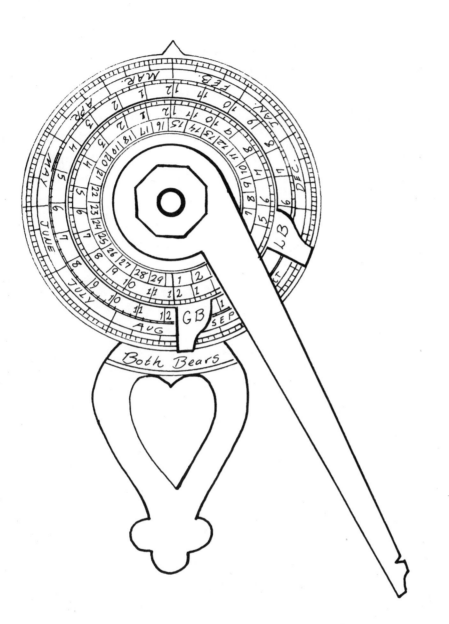

Figure 8-1
The nocturnal.

more advanced clocks of its day, and so remained in use up until the early 19th century, many years after the chronometer was perfected. Its only serious limitation seems to have been that to function at all, Polaris had to be visible. The nocturnal was useless in overcast skies and would not work south of the equator, where Polaris lies below the horizon.

Only after Bowditch developed accurate latitude corrections, and after accurate sea clocks and chronometers became affordable, was the nocturnal finally rendered obsolete.

This project is a near-replica of a sea nocturnal in common use in the 18th century. It can read time from either the Little Bear or the Great Bear to within a few minutes. The hour face and latitude-correction face have been updated to the late 20th century.

Figure 8-2
Nocturnal base and pointer.

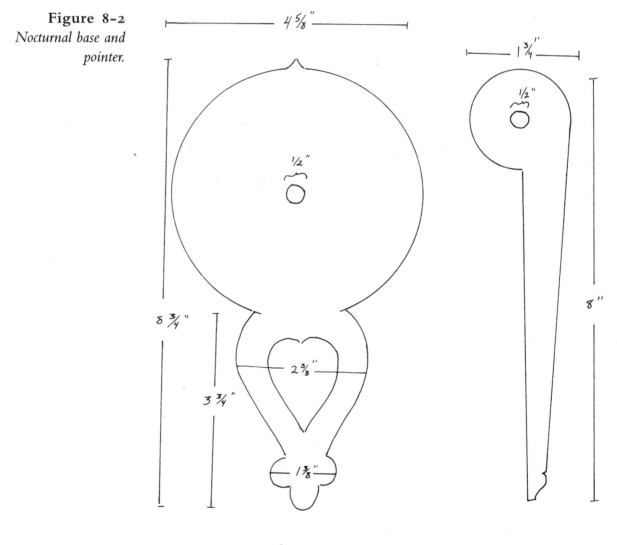

base

pointer

Making a Nocturnal

Here's what you'll need:

- One piece hardwood or plywood, ³⁄₁₆" × 6" × 12"
- Copper tubing, ½" outside diameter, 1' long
- One sheet parchment paper
- Two brass washers, ½" inside diameter, 1" outside diameter

Using a compass and ruler, draw the nocturnal's individual components: the base, hour disk, pointer, and two pivot endpieces. Draw

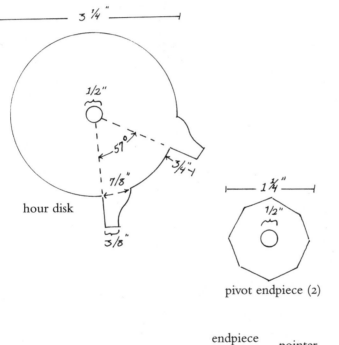

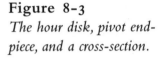

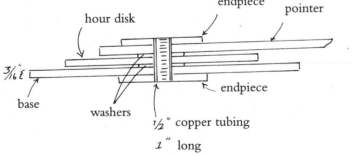

Figure 8-3
The hour disk, pivot endpiece, and a cross-section.

Figure 8-4
The date face.

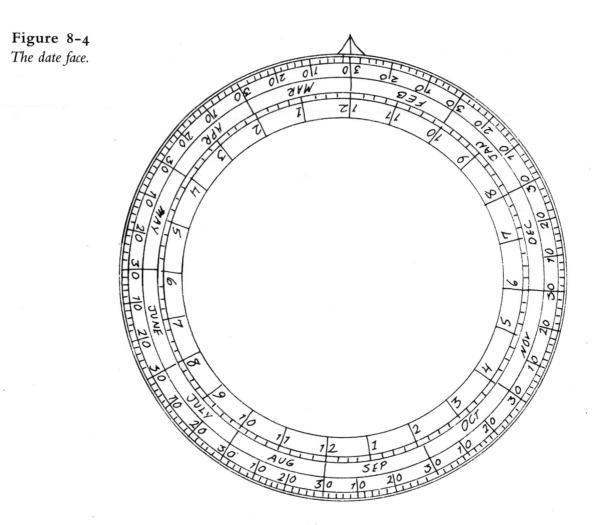

them full-sized and transfer them to the wood using carbon paper. Also, transfer the mark left by the compass point at the center of each piece. Cut the pieces out using a scroll saw or coping saw and drill a ½-inch hole through each center mark.

This nocturnal has three faces. One is on the back. The face of the date disk, reading from the outermost circle to the innermost, shows days, months, quarter-hours, and hours. Twelve midnight is uppermost on the disk, just beneath March 1.

The hour disk, also reading inward, shows quarter-hours, hours, and the days of the lunar month, from new moon to new moon.

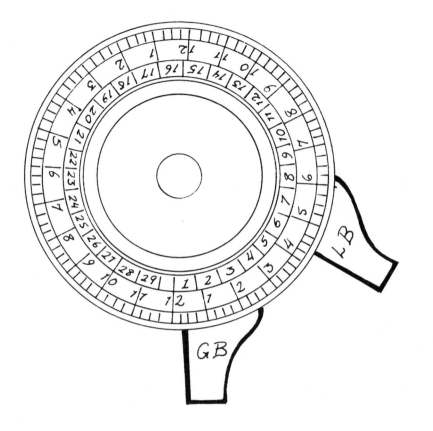

Figure 8-5
The hour face.

Correcting Latitude
*To find corrections for a Polar
Star sight, hold the nocturnal so
the latitude-correction circles face
you. As with a time sight, locate
Polaris through the center hole,
extend your arm until the
Pointer or Guardian stars are
visible, and rotate the pointer
until its unnotched edge lines up
with one of these pairs of stars.*

*You can read the time correc-
tion by noting where the
unnotched edge of the pointer
arm crosses the circles. These corrections are in minutes of arc.
There are 60 minutes in one
degree. See Figure 8-6.*

*If you are sighting on the
Great Bear, use the inner circle.
If you are sighting on the Little
Bear, use the outer circle. Then
simply add or subtract the reading on the nocturnal from what-
ever latitude is being shown on
your quadrant, astrolabe, or other
instrument.*

*For instance if your quadrant
shows a latitude of 37 degrees
and your nocturnal reads 45, add
45 minutes to your latitude to
get 37 degrees 45 minutes. Where
a minus sign precedes the correction, subtract that number of
minutes from your reading.*

On the back of the instrument is a face with two circles of latitude
corrections. The outer circle is for the Great Bear and the inner is for the
Little Bear. Corrections are given in minutes. The phrase "Both Bears"
on the handle of the nocturnal refers to this latitude-correction diagram.

Unless you are an experienced engraver, drawing the date, hour,
and latitude-correction faces on parchment paper is far easier than trying to engrave all the increments directly on wood.

All the faces in this chapter are drawn full-sized, so the easiest way
to make the faces is to photocopy them onto parchment paper. Glue
the paper faces to the disks with Elmer's Glue-All and protect them

Figure 8-6
Latitude-correction circles.

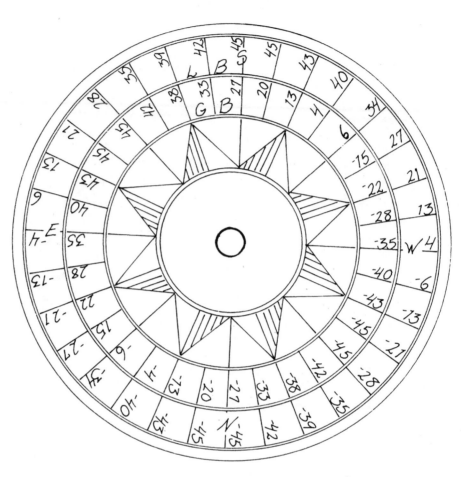

Figure 8-7
*Finding the time from the
Great Bear.*

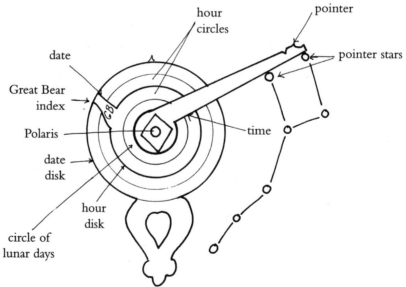

LATITUDE HOOKS AND AZIMUTH RINGS

with several coats of shellac. Take an X-Acto knife and carefully remove the paper covering the center holes.

To assemble the nocturnal, first roughen the last ⅜₆ inch of both ends of the copper pivot tube with sandpaper. Then, using epoxy, glue one end of the tube into the hole of one of the endpieces. After the epoxy has thoroughly cured, insert the tube through the holes in the pointer, hour disk, and base.

Now glue the remaining endpiece to the end of the tube with a small dab of epoxy. Be careful not to glue the pivot to the other disks. The hour disk and pointer arm should turn freely, but not too loosely. Once the epoxy cures, finish your nocturnal with beeswax polish.

Using Your Nocturnal

To use your nocturnal, rotate the hour disk until either of two small indices—marked GB for Great Bear and LB for Little Bear—is aligned with the date on the date circle. Then hold it upright, facing you, and sight Polaris through the pivot.

I have found that the best way to read a nocturnal is to bring the sight close to your eye, find Polaris, and then slowly extend your arm until Kochab or the Pointers come into view. It's best to keep both eyes open while doing this.

If you've set the Great Bear index to match the date, line up the unnotched edge of the pointer arm with the Pointers of the Great Bear (Dubhe and Mirek). If you're using the Little Bear index, put the pointer arm in line with the Guards of the Little Bear (Kochab and Pherkad)—see Figure 8-8.

You can then read the time on the hour disk by noting where the unnotched edge of the pointer crosses the hour circle. It can be accurate to within a quarter-hour. The time shown in Figure 8-1, for example, is 2:15.

One final word: Remember to hold the nocturnal upright. Its accuracy depends on this.

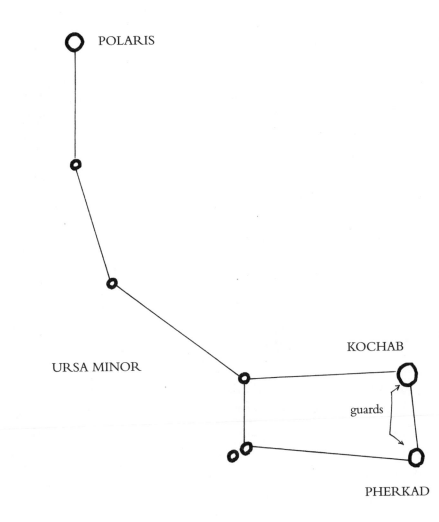

Figure 8-8
Locating the Guards of the Little Bear.

CHAPTER

9 The Cross-Staff

Centuries before mariners navigated with it, the cross-staff, like the quadrant and astrolabe, was used by astronomers to measure the angles between stars, planets, and other celestial bodies, as well as to determine latitudes and heights. The man who probably deserves the credit as the first to use the cross-staff as a navigation tool is the German mathematician and navigator Martin Behaim, who sailed with the Portuguese explorer Diogo Cão on his second voyage down the coast of Africa in 1485. Behaim is also known for adapting the astrolabe to celestial navigation.

The cross-staff, also known as the Jacob's staff, consists of a long, square hardwood staff, often made of rosewood or ebony, and a shorter crosspiece, or transom, that slides up and down the staff. When the staff is held up to the eye and the crosspiece is adjusted to fill the apparent distance between Polaris or the sun and the horizon, a graduated scale on one edge of the staff shows the angular measurement.

Because it could be used by one person, the cross-staff was a much handier device than the quadrant or astrolabe, and was much simpler and more accurate all around. Nonetheless, it was still prone to error from ocular parallax because it required a navigator to look in two places at once. Another problem was that navigators were forced to

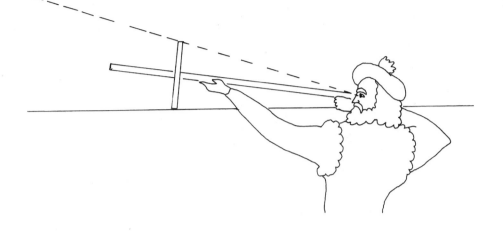

Figure 9-1
The cross-staff.

look directly into the sun when taking a sun sight. Waiting for a cloudy day might save them from being blinded by the sun's glare, but then the horizon was often obscured.

In time, cross-staffs became highly developed and elaborate instruments. To improve the consistency of sightings, some cross-staffs had pinnule sights: one ocular near the eye and two objectives, one at either end of the crosspiece. Sometimes these pinnules were fitted with smoked glass to reduce glare.

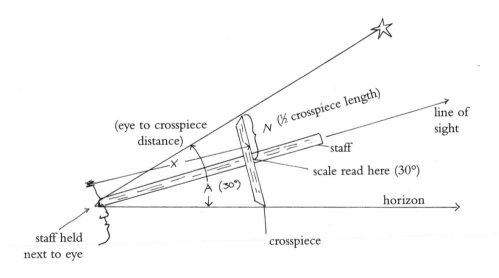

Figure 9-2
How the cross-staff works.

$$\text{TAN } A = \frac{n}{x}$$

Other cross-staffs had as many as four crosspieces of different lengths (for use in higher or lower latitudes) and four different scales, one on each face of the staff. I've seen one such cross-staff that was 36 inches long and had a set of four crosspieces that were 4¾ inches, 5⅝ inches, 12⅝ inches and 23½ inches long. These were referred to as the 10-, 30-, 60-, and 90-degree crosspieces, respectively.

Making a Cross-Staff

Here's what you'll need:

- One piece hardwood, 1" × 1" × 48"
- One piece hardwood, ¼" × 1" × 4½"
- Eight brass screws, ⅜" long

Your stock should be dry, vertical-grain lumber, which is less likely to warp. To make the staff, rip a 36-inch length of stock with a table saw so it is ¾ inch square in section and absolutely straight and uniform in width.

The length of the crosspiece will depend on where the cross-staff will be used. For Polaris sights, longer crosspieces are needed in higher latitudes; shorter crosspieces are necessary for lower latitudes. The following chart shows the best crosspiece lengths when sighting Polaris with a 36-inch staff.

Latitude in degrees	Crosspiece length
0-10	2 inches
10-20	4 inches
20-30	6 inches
30-40	8 inches
40-50	10 inches
50 or more	12 inches

When taking sun sights, this rule of thumb is reversed. At the equator, for instance, you'd need a crosspiece as long as 2 feet to mea-

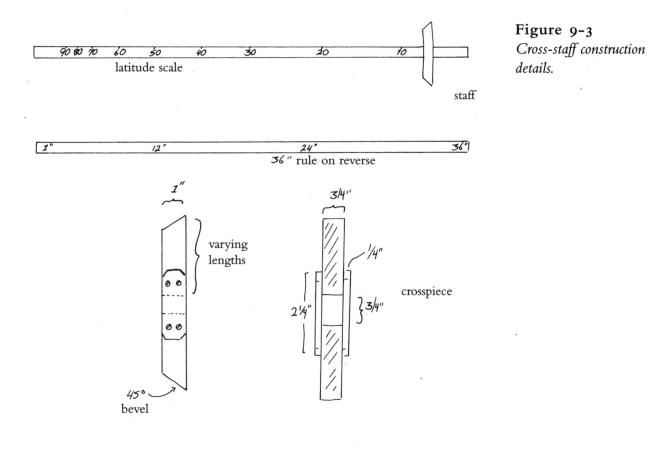

Figure 9-3
Cross-staff construction details.

latitude scale

staff

36" rule on reverse

varying lengths

bevel

crosspiece

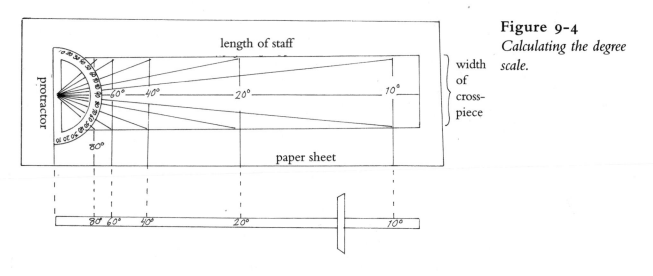

Figure 9-4
Calculating the degree scale.

length of staff

width of cross-piece

protractor

paper sheet

Stand facing the star you wish to sight, place the butt of the staff against your cheekbone so your eye sights along the center of the staff's side, and raise the other end of the staff midway between the horizon and the star.

Slide the crosspiece forward or backward until it appears to just touch the horizon and the star.

If you are sighting the sun, split its disk in half. Use a safety monocle while you do this, or a special pair of sunglasses designed to allow you to look directly at the sun for a brief period. Ordinary sunglasses are not safe. To be sure, consult an optometrist.

Where the forward edge of the crosspiece crosses the staff, you can read the altitude from the degree scale.

Measuring distances

The cross-staff is also a handy piloting tool. For instance, if you know the height or width of an object, perhaps from a chart, then the cross-staff can tell you how far away it is. That's because the ratio of the size of an object to its distance from the observer is the same as the length of the crosspiece to the distance from the eye to the crosspiece.

(continued on page 73)

Figure 9-5
Finding distance from an island of known length.

sure the sun's 90-degree height at the equinoxes. At higher latitudes, shorter crosspieces are adequate. Also, the seasonal variation in the sun's height means you'll need longer crosspieces in the summer and shorter crosspieces in the winter.

The following instructions are for a cross-staff with a 10-inch crosspiece. If you need to make a crosspiece longer than 10 inches, you'll need more than 48 inches of lumber.

Rip two ¼-inch-by-2¼-inch strips out of the one-inch stock, then rip the remaining stock down to a ¾-inch square section, just like the staff. To save wood, cut the crosspiece in two at a 45-degree angle; this produces two beveled ends in one pass.

Trim square the ends that will slide along the staff. Glue the strips to the transom pieces, as shown, with wood glue or resorcinol glue, and fasten with brass screws. The assembled crosspiece has to be straight on all sides and should slide easily on the staff without wobbling. Staff and crosspiece may now be stained or painted.

The degree scale of the cross-staff can be calculated with this trigonometric equation: the tangent of the altitude (A) equals one-half the crosspiece length (N) divided by the eye-to-crosspiece distance (X). See Figure 9-2.

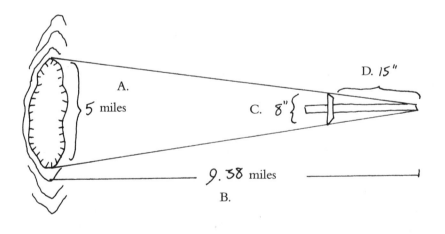

$$A : B = C : D$$

LATITUDE HOOKS AND AZIMUTH RINGS

Cross-staff markings can also be determined graphically using a large sheet of paper and a protractor graduated in half-degrees. Draw a rectangle 36 inches long and as wide as the crosspiece, then draw a line down the center of its length. Tape the protractor as shown in Figure 9-4, with its centerpoint and 90-degree mark on the centerline.

Now draw radial lines from the protractor's centerpoint to the edges of the rectangle. Perpendiculars drawn from the points where the radial lines intersect the rectangle edges cross the centerline where the cross-staff degree markings should be located. For instance, radial lines drawn through the 50-degree marks on either side of the protractor create an angle of 80 degrees, or twice the difference between 90 degrees and 50 degrees.

Once the centerline is marked for each degree between one and 90 (note that they will not be evenly spaced), simply lay the staff on the paper alongside the centerline and mark the face of the staff with a pencil. Use a square to ensure your marks on the staff are square to the edge. Then go over the pencil markings with pen and ink and write in the numerals. If you want, make a paper degree scale instead, glue it to the staff with Elmer's Glue-All, and cover it with several coats of shellac.

If you wish to find your distance from, say, an island having a charted length of 5 miles, and the 8-inch crosspiece shows 15 inches on the 36-inch scale when its ends line up with either end of the island, then the distance equals the island's length (5) times the staff's scale (15) divided by the crosspiece length (8), which equals 9.38 miles. Note that this is the distance to a spot midway between the two points on the island, not to the near shore.

The same procedure will tell you your distance from an object of known height. For example, if you take a sight of a lighthouse with an elevation of 300 feet and your 8-inch crosspiece rests on the staff's 30-inch mark, then the distance to the lighthouse equals 300 times 30 divided by 8, or 1,125 feet.

Remember that when measuring something in feet, the calculated distance using the ratios will also be in feet. If you wish, you can convert to nautical miles afterward by dividing the calculated distance by 6,076.

You can also use your cross-staff, instead of your sextant or compass, for day-to-day pilotage, finding your distance off headlands by doubling the angle on the bow, for example.

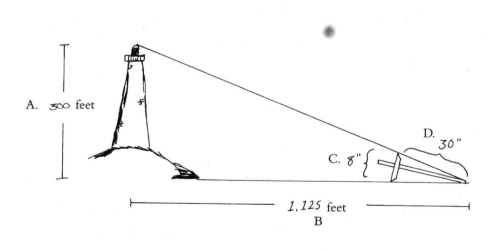

A. 300 feet

B. 1,125 feet

C. 8"

D. 30"

A : B = C : D

Figure 9-6
Finding distance from an object of known height.

On the opposite side of the staff, inscribe ¼-inch gradations from a yardstick, with the 1-inch mark being closest to the eye. This scale is used in piloting to find the distances from objects of a known size and the heights of objects at a known distance.

In an emergency, a cross-staff can be cobbled together from any two pieces of wood held perpendicular to each other; measurements can then be taken with a ruler or tape measure.

The Backstaff

Tʜᴇ ʙᴀᴄᴋꜱᴛᴀғғ ɪꜱ ᴛʜᴇ ғɪʀꜱᴛ ɴᴀᴠɪɢᴀᴛɪᴏɴᴀʟ instrument invented by a seaman whose name we know: John Davis, an English explorer of the late 16th century. Though Davis is almost unknown today, his various accomplishments should place him at the forefront of historically important navigators. He wrote an important *rutter*, a book of nautical instructions called *The Seaman's Secrets*, and unsuccessfully sought the Northwest Passage. Davis Strait between Baffin Island and Greenland is named for him, but not by him.

Davis was impressed with the accuracy of the cross-staff (Chapter 9), but wanted to find a way to eliminate the "uncertainty" of the instrument due to the "disorderly placing of the staff to the eye." He experimented with a number of different designs, including a staff with a sliding arc, before hitting upon this concept around 1590. His device, also known as the Davis or English quadrant, was so practical and so elegantly simple that it remained in use—little changed—for more than two hundred years .

Basically, the backstaff consists of three vanes—a sight vane, a shadow vane, and a horizon vane—and a pair of arcs attached to a staff and marked in degrees. The sight vane slides along the sight arc; the shadow vane slides along the shadow arc. These arcs are sections of two

Figure 10-1
The backstaff.

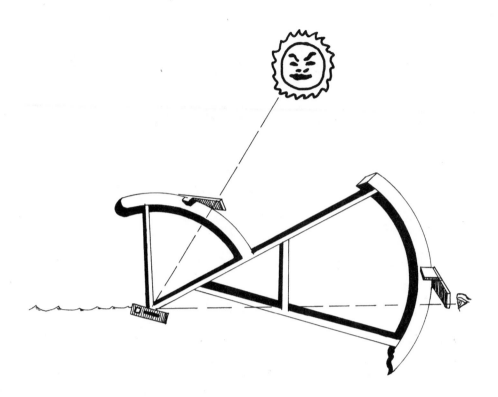

concentric circles whose center is the location of the horizon vane. The small arc measures 60 degrees, and the large one measures 30 degrees. Added together, they yield the maximum zenith altitude of 90 degrees.

Backstaffs were often built of ebony or rosewood. The arcs were commonly of boxwood, which is well suited to engraving. Some early American instruments are made entirely of fruitwood such as pear.

Compared with the old cross-staff, the backstaff had several advantages. A navigator could stand with the sun over his shoulder (thus the name backstaff), so glare was eliminated. Also, because the backstaff brought the sun's shadow into direct line with the horizon, there were no parallax errors. In fact, the backstaff made possible a quantum leap in navigational accuracy, as significant an improvement in its time as satellite navigation systems have been in ours. Suddenly, navigators who had been satisfied with an accuracy measured in degrees could find where they were at sea within a minute of a degree, which translates to one sea mile. And in contrast to the cross-staff, they could use the same backstaff at different latitudes in either hemisphere.

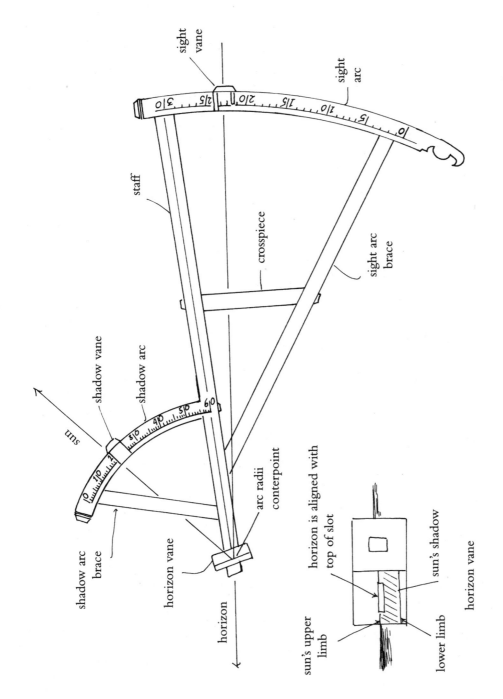

Figure 10-2
Parts of the backstaff.

THE BACKSTAFF **77**

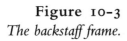

Figure 10-3
The backstaff frame.

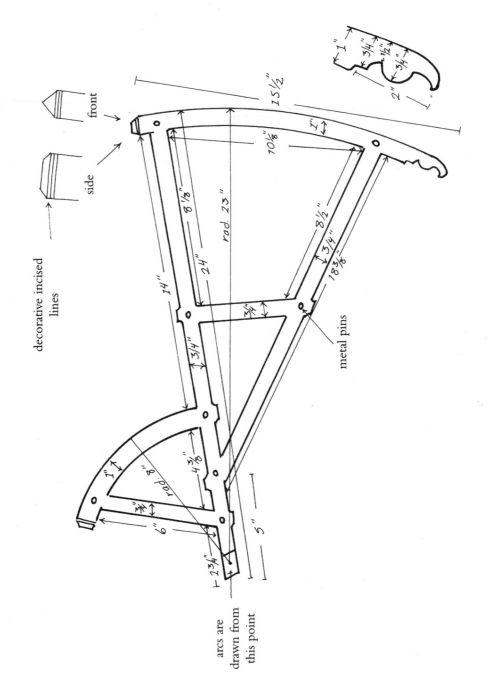

Originally, the backstaff was used only for noon sights to find latitude, but later, the mirror backstaff was developed to measure the altitude of stars and planets, which don't cast shadows. The instrument worked so well that until the advent of the octant in 1731, and in some cases even later, the mirror backstaff was the primary tool of celestial navigation.

Making a Backstaff

Here's what you'll need:

- One piece hardwood plywood, ½" × 16" × 25" OR
- One piece hardwood, ½" × 26" × 8"
- One brass rod, ³⁄₁₆" × 6" OR
- Eight flathead brass screws, 1" long
- Three pieces mahogany, 1" × 2" × 4"
- Two pieces .025" sheet brass, ¼" × 1"

The first step in building the backstaff is to choose your material. A backstaff made of hardwood is more traditional, but entails lots of precise, time-consuming cutting and fitting. A plywood backstaff can be cut out quickly, but will not have the classic look of a solid-wood instrument.

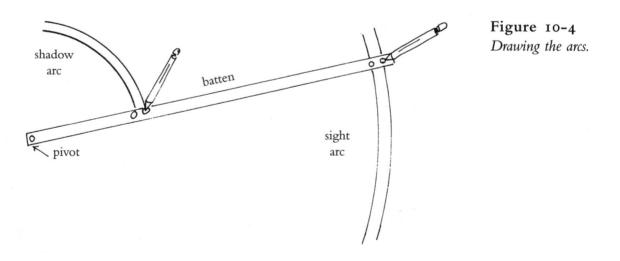

Figure 10-4
Drawing the arcs.

Whichever material you choose, you'll first have to make a full-sized pattern or set of patterns for the frame, following the dimensions given in Figure 10-3. The pattern for the plywood backstaff can be drawn right on the wood. For the solid-wood backstaff, draw the frame full-size on paper. Then take the measurements for the individual pieces directly from the paper or transfer the patterns to your stock with carbon paper. There will be six parts in all: staff, sight arc, sight-arc brace, shadow arc, shadow-arc brace, and crosspiece.

The best way to draw each arc accurately is to use a 25-inch wooden batten with a ⅛-inch pivot hole drilled ½ inch from one end—see Figure 10-4. Then drill holes with centers exactly 7, 8, 22, and 23 inches from the pivot point. Tap a small finish nail through the pivot hole and scribe the inside and outside of each arc with a pencil. You can use the same method to draw the paper degree scales for the arcs.

Once your pattern is on the plywood, cut out the stock with a sabersaw and a fine blade. Take your time; plywood splits and mars easily. Sand and finish as you wish.

Figure 10-5
Exploded view of the hardwood backstaff frame.

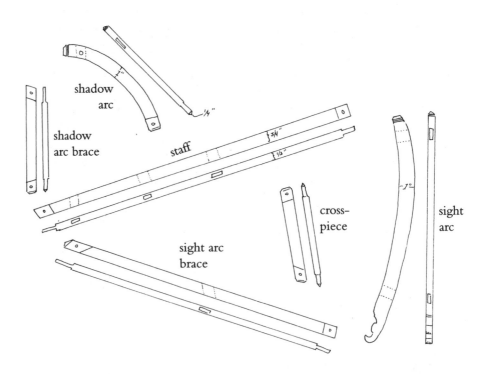

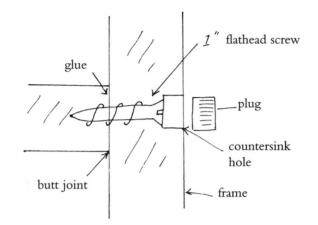

glue

1" flathead screw

plug

countersink hole

butt joint

frame

Figure 10-6
Screw-and-glue reinforced butt joints.

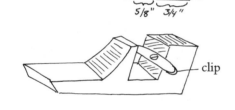

4"

1/4"

45° bevel

5/8"   3/4"

1 1/4"

.025 brass clip

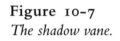

1"

3 1/4"

1/2" screw

Figure 10-7
The shadow vane.

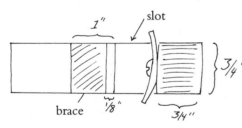

clip

shadow arc

vane

1"

slot

brace   1/8"

3/4"

3/4"

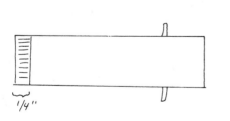

1/4"

For a hardwood frame, cut out the arcs with a scrollsaw or saber-saw; use a table saw for the straight members. The original instruments were constructed with mortise-and-tenon joints. Should you decide to use mortise-and-tenon joints, Figure 10-5 shows you where to cut them. Carefully fashion the mortises with a mortise chisel and cut the tenons with a hand saw.

In the traditional backstaff, the tenons commonly protrude from the frame by a small amount, ending in a peaked crown. Glue the mortise-and-tenon frame pieces together with wood glue, then run ³⁄₁₆-inch brass pegs—cut from a brass rod—through the tenons.

However, with modern adhesives you don't need such complex joinery. Epoxied butt joints (Figure 10-6) reinforced with brass screws have great strength, and once the screw heads are covered with wooden plugs, the frame is hard to distinguish from one made with traditional joinery.

Trace the shadow vane pattern in Figure 10-7 onto one of the ¼-inch pieces of mahogany and cut out the rough shape with a coping saw. You will need wood knives and chisels for fine work, as well as a small file and sanding block to shape the ⅜-inch slot where the vane fits over the shadow arc. The vane is held to the arc with a 1-inch × ¼-inch brass clip bent slightly to maintain a friction fit. Attach the clip to the inside of the vane's slot using a ½-inch flathead screw and a dab of epoxy. Drive the screw into this slot with the side of a screwdriver bit or the square edge of a knife.

The sight vane (Figure 10-8) is similar to the shadow vane, except that its triangular brace is half as thick. Drill the ⅛-inch sight hole through the middle of the vane's outer leg. Notice how the sight hole and the edge of the half brace line up. You read the arc scale where this edge of the half brace crosses it. When the vane is attached to the sight arc, this edge of the half brace marks where the arc scale is read.

Sand and finish both vanes with stain and varnish.

To make the horizon vane, take your last piece of ¼-inch by 2-inch mahogany stock and cut a ⅜-inch-deep by 2-inch-wide rabbet across its width. Then trim the rabbeted edge to a 45-degree bevel. A glued mortise-and-tenon joint holds this vane to the frame. Chisel this

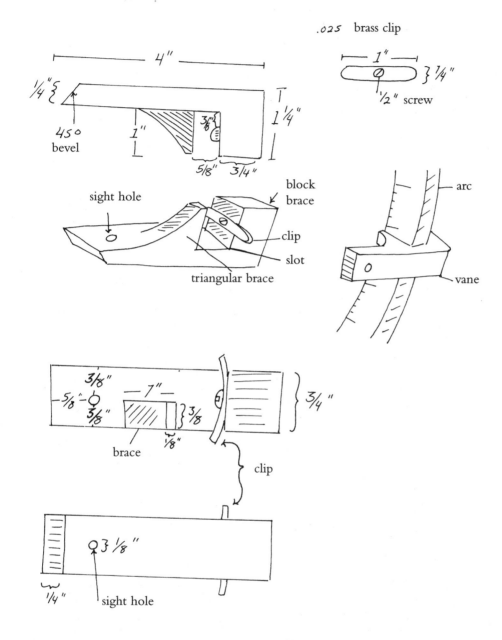

Figure 10-8
The sight vane.

mortise and the horizon slot at the same angle: 64 degrees from the face of the vane, as shown in Figure 10-9. When the vane is fitted in place, it should cant upward 116 degrees from the centerline of the staff, and the top of its horizon slot on the side nearest the navigator should line up with the centerpoint of both arcs.

Figure 10-9
The horizon vane.

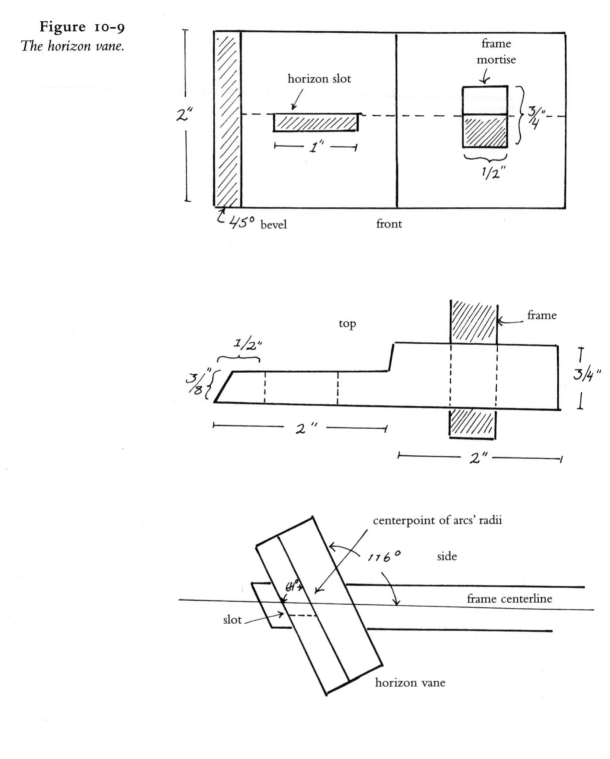

You can glue the paper arc scales to the frame with Elmer's Glue-All, or you can transfer the degree markings from paper to frame with carbon paper and then ink or engrave the wood directly. The original instruments had engraved arcs. Note that both the 60-degree mark on the shadow-arc scale and the 30-degree mark on the sight-arc scale fall on the centerline of the staff. Finish with two or three coats of shellac.

Sometimes two arcs were engraved on the shadow arc—one 0 to 60 degrees from left to right (as shown in Figure 10-2) and another underneath reading in the opposite direction, from 60 to 0 degrees. This allowed both the altitude (bottom scale) and the zenith distance (top scale) to be measured in one sight.

As you sand your backstaff in preparation for finishing, be sure to round off any sharp edges and soften the lines a little. This instrument was meant for workaday navigation and should be comfortable in the hand.

Once the sight and shadow vanes are set in place and the wood is polished with beeswax, your backstaff is ready for use or display.

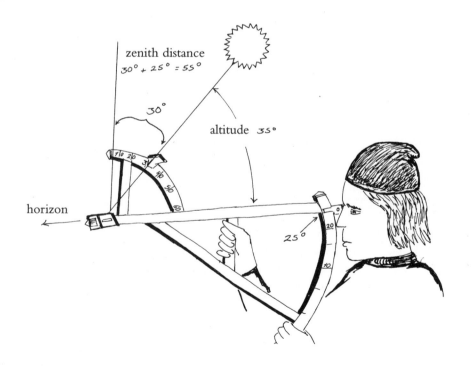

Figure 10-10
The backstaff in use.

CHAPTER 11 The Dry-Card Compass

Not only is the compass one of the oldest navigational tools, it is still one of the most widely used navigational instruments in the world today. The Greeks or the Chinese were probably the first to discover that certain rocks called *lodestones*—a strongly magnetic type of the mineral magnetite—always lined up north and south when allowed to turn freely. The Vikings were among the first seafarers to use lodestones to find north. They rested their lodestones on boards floating in buckets of water. The modern compass, with its card turning smoothly in its dampening bath of light mineral oil, operates on the same basic principle of magnetic attraction.

Early Chinese compasses used fixed cards and moving iron pointers, not too different from today's pocket compass. The Chinese divided the compass card into 24 points instead of the European 32.

The Western system came about from the common association of winds with direction. The cardinal compass points were referred to as the north, south, east, and west winds. These were further divided into halfwinds, such as northeast and southwest; quarterwinds, such as north-northwest and east-southeast; and finally the 32 winds of the wind rose. Eventually the wind rose became the compass rose.

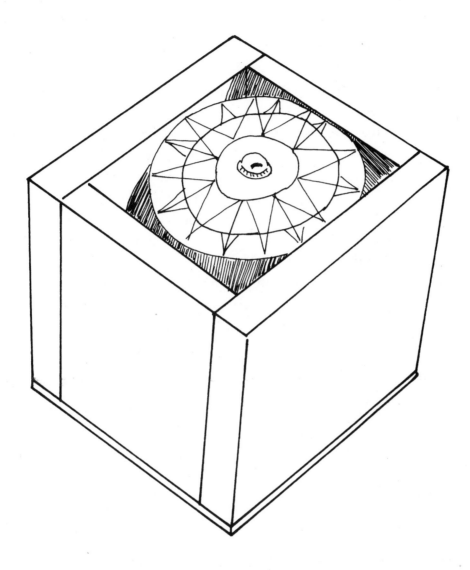

Figure 11-1
The compass.

Figure 11-2
An early compass.

Using Your Compass

If you use this compass aboard a boat, place the box so that an imaginary line from the center pivot of the compass through the lubber line runs exactly fore-and-aft. If it's not convenient to place the box on the exact fore-and-aft line running from the bow to the middle of the stern, the compass will work equally well if you set up the box parallel to that line. When you're under way, the compass point closest to the lubber line shows your boat's heading.

If your card is detailed enough to let you extrapolate degrees, you can take bearings by sighting across the center of the compass to a charted object and noting the reading at the edge of the card.

If you have a nautical almanac, a bearing of the sun at nautical sunset or sunrise (when the disc is half its diameter above the horizon) will give you your latitude from simple tables.

To calculate your local variation, find Polaris, drop a perpendicular to the horizon (the pilot's blessing mentioned above) and aim the lubber line at that spot. Note the reading on your compass, the number of degrees showing at the lubber line. The difference between that and 360 degrees is your local variation. If, for example, you get a lubber line reading of 340

(continued on page 89)

The compass rose on the early instruments was a movable card with magnetized bars of soft iron mounted on its underside. This card turned on a pivot and was not submerged in water or oil, hence the name dry-card compass. Early compass roses didn't show letter abbreviations of the compass points. This was mainly because most mariners were illiterate. Sailors were expected to know the points and to recite them from memory, a practice known as boxing the compass.

To discover whether the compass needed remagnetizing, a navigator would use a technique called the pilot's blessing. Facing north, he would bring his hand up flat between his eyes, and align it with Polaris. Then he would drop his hand straight down to the compass face and check against north on the compass rose. If the compass erred, the pilot remagnetized the bars by rubbing them with a piece of lodestone or by moving the stone in circles around the entire compass.

This blessing was also used to find local variation, the compass's divergence from true north. Unfortunately, the magnetic north pole does not coincide with the geographic north pole. The amount of variation differs according to your location. It can be a significant amount—often more than 25 degrees. There is evidence that Columbus knew about variation, but did not understand it well enough to prevent a small southwesterly error creeping into his track across the Atlantic.

The base of the compass was commonly a wooden box or bowl designed to protect the card from wind and weather. The card pivoted on a sharply pointed wire to keep it level as the ship pitched and heeled. Later, compass containers were fitted with a double set of gimbals that allowed the card to remain stable no matter how much the ship rolled.

The lubber line on the compass box, together with the central pivot of the compass card, simply represented the fore-and-aft line of the vessel and was always set up parallel to it. The helmsman used the lubber line to hold a course. As long as the desired heading on the compass card lay next to the lubber line, the ship was on its course.

Simple dry-card compasses were still in common use early in this century. And though not as accurate as modern oil-filled compasses because of friction in the pivot, they can still be found in areas where traditional sailors have survived.

The following project is modeled after a Portuguese compass of 1402.

Making a Dry-Card Compass

Here's what you'll need:

- One piece hardwood, ¾" × 3½" × 22"
- One piece hardwood, ½" × 5¾" × 5½"
- 16 bronze nails, 1¼" long
- One piece .005" sheet brass, 1¼" square
- One piece copper or brass wire, 1⁄16" diameter
- Art paper or parchment paper
- Six sewing needles, 1⅛" long
- White card stock, 4" × 4" (about the same weight as an index card)

The first step in making this compass is to build the box. You'll note that all fastenings are non-ferrous. Steel or iron would affect the compass.

Take your ¾-inch stock—mahogany is a good choice—and cut it into five sections: two 5¾-inch pieces, two 4-inch pieces, and one 1½-inch piece. The matching pairs will be the sides of the box. Trim the 1½-inch piece to make a block 1½ inches × 1½ inches and drill a ⅜-inch deep pilot hole in the center of one face with a finish nail. Glue this block, which holds the compass card's pivot wire, to the exact center of the ½-inch stock, which will be the bottom of the box.

Assemble the box as shown with wood glue and 1¼-inch bronze nails. Finish the box with paint or stain and varnish, then engrave a lubber line in the center of one of the top edges of the box.

Epoxy a straight, stiff, 2½-inch piece of brass or copper wire into the hole in the block at the bottom of the box after filing the wire's exposed end to a sharp point so the compass card's pivot will turn freely on it.

degrees, your compass's north marker is obviously 20 degrees to the right of true north as shown by Polaris. So your variation is 20 degrees east. This correction can be applied to all compass sights to convert magnetic bearings to true bearings, or vice versa.

If the north marker is to the left of Polaris, your variation is west. You can gauge the accuracy of your compass by checking the variation you find against the actual variation, which is shown on a nautical chart or survey map.

You may be able to plot the position of your home on a chart or map by taking two or more bearings of recognizable charted objects. But while you're taking bearings—at home or aboard ship—beware of tin cans, metallic objects, and electronic gear, particularly radio loudspeakers, which will throw your compass off. Even metal in the frames of your glasses will affect the compass reading, if the metal contains iron or steel. To be safe, keep any ferrous material six feet away or more.

Try to get three bearings for a "fix" of your home. Most often, they won't cross over each other at one point, as they should in theory. Usually, they'll form a small triangle or "cocked hat," as navigators call it. The smaller your cocked hat, the more accurate your compass.

Figure 11-3
*Compass box
construction details.*

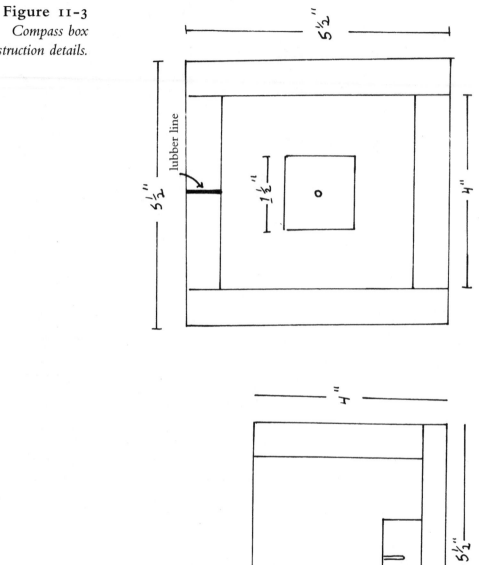

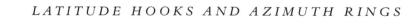

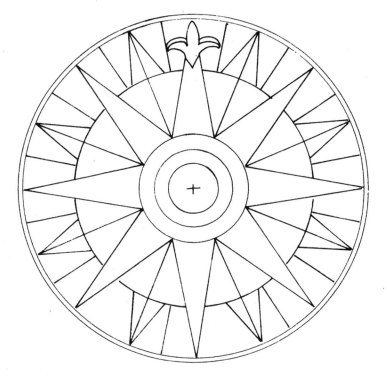

Figure 11-4
A traditional compass card.

The next step is to draw your compass rose. First, photocopy the compass rose (Figure 11-4) and trace the design onto the card stock using a light table. An art pen and compass will help you draw the circles and compass points. Take an X-Acto knife and cut out the rose and the innermost circle with the cross at the center.

Now remove the photocopy, turn the card over on the light table, and draw a line from the north point of the rose to the south point. Then draw parallel pencil lines ½ inch, ⅞ inch, and 1¼ inches from either side of this north/south line.

Turn the card over again and paint the rose with watercolors following the color scheme in Figure 11-5. Use red and blue for alternate points and gold for north.

To make the compass's pivot, cut a 1¼-inch diameter circle out of the .005-inch sheet brass with a pair of scissors. Cut a quarter-slice out of the circle, bring the two corners together to form a cone, and glue the cone's edge with epoxy. After it cures, epoxy the pivot cone's rim and glue the cone over the circle near the center of the compass rose.

You could also use an aluminum thimble from a fabric store as a pivot. To preserve a nautical flavor, file off the dimples on the outside of the thimble with a single-cut file.

The magnets in this compass are actually six magnetized sewing needles. All you do is lightly stroke each needle from eye to point with a bar magnet; a common refrigerator-door magnet will do fine. A

Figure 11-5
A suggested coloring key.

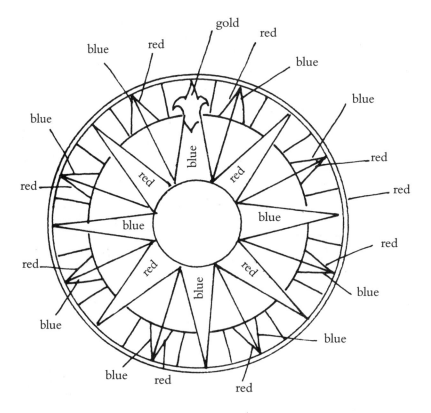

Figure 11-6
Construction of the brass pivot.

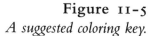

1 ¼"

90°

sheet brass disk

cone

glued edge

epoxy cone to compass card

cut out

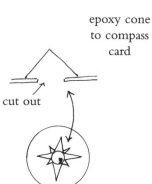

dozen or so strokes for each needle should be sufficient to make the needle's sharp end point north.

Use one end of the bar magnet to stroke the full length of each needle, lifting it up high for the return stroke and bringing it back down again for the beginning of the magnetizing stroke.

Float one needle on a cork in water to see if the sharp end of the

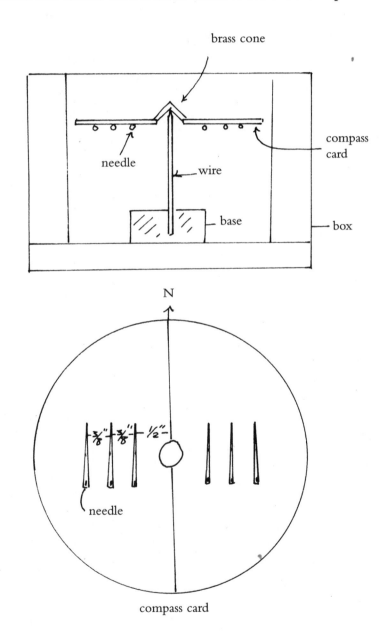

Figure 11-7
Fixing the magnetized needles.

needle points north. If it points south instead, go through the procedure again, using the opposite end of the bar magnet.

Line up the magnetized needles with the parallel lines on the underside of the card—points pointing north—and affix them with epoxy.

Rest the compass card's pivot on the upright wire in the box. The compass should point north. If not, you may have to add more magnetized needles or a pair of small (½ inch × ¼ inch) permanent bar magnets to the underside of the card. To find these bar magnets' south poles (which are attracted to the Earth's nortj889h pole) float them as you did the needles, or put them in a plastic lid in a bowl of water, away from any magnetic influences. Mark the ends that point north.

You will have to remagnetize the needles periodically because they gradually lose their magnetism.

The Traverse Board

CHAPTER

12

FOR SAILING CRAFT, THE COURSE FROM STARTING POINT to destination is rarely a straight line, especially when traveling to windward. A sailing ship zigzags through a series of *tacks*, or traverses, on different *rhumb lines*, or direction lines. (A rhumb is any one of the 32 points of the compass, or the sector of arc between between two consecutive points.)

To plot the ship's position on a chart, the navigator needs to know exactly how many zigs and zags were made. It's also necessary to know how far the ship traveled on each leg, and in what direction.

This information came from a traverse board, or travas, a simple, ancient device for recording a ship's speed and direction. A traverse board is nothing more than a wooden board with a compass rose on its face and 32 radial rows of holes. Each row has eight holes and corresponds to a point on the compass. Later, a grid was added to record speed. The board stood near the helm, and like the compass, could be used by illiterate sailors.

Early navigators relied so heavily on rhumb-line navigating that their charts were marked not in latitude and longitude but in rhumb lines originating from various wind roses. At first, the changes in a ship's latitude and longitude were solved trigonometrically using plane right

Figure 12-1
The traverse board.

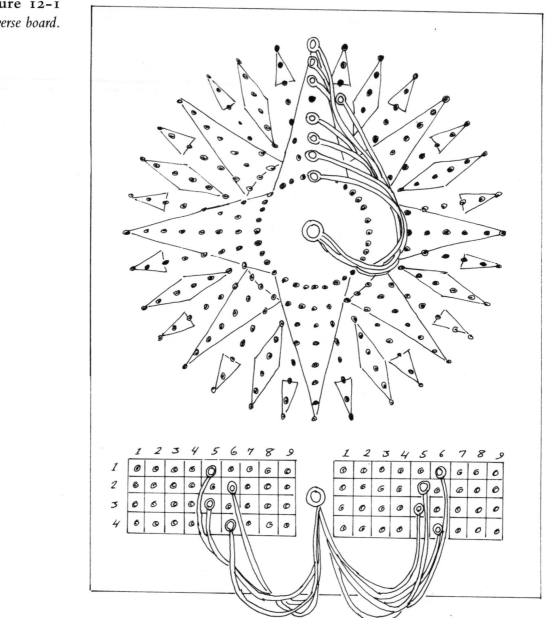

triangles. Later, to simplify calculations, traverse tables were published, and charts often had a small set in the corner.

Plotting a course in this manner is called plane sailing because it assumes, for simplicity's sake, that the Earth is flat. It works well in low latitudes and over short distances.

Making a Traverse Board

Here's what you'll need:

- One hardwood or softwood board (not plywood), ¾" × 12" × 16"
- One hardwood dowel, ½" × 3"
- One hardwood dowel, ³⁄₁₆" × 18"
- Lightweight string, 10'8" long

To draw the compass rose, you'll need a compass, a ruler, a protractor with half-degree graduations, and a sharp pencil. First, find a point 6 inches below the center of the board's top edge (its 12-inch edge), and from that point lightly draw a 10-inch-diameter circle—radius 5 inches. Now, reducing the radius by a half-inch each time, draw seven concentric circles inside the large circle. The innermost circle will be 3 inches across. Lay your protractor along a line that bisects the circle vertically and line up the protractor's center with the centerpoint of the circles. Now mark off the points of the compass, which are exactly 11¼ degrees apart, so that 4 points equal 45 degrees. You may find it easier to mark the cardinal points first, then the half-points and quarter-points. A pair of dividers stepped along the perimeter will help you to halve and quarter the gradations with precision.

You need only mark the rhumbs for one side of your circle. Now draw radial lines from the perimeter, through the centerpoint to the other perimeter. Incidentally, make light pencil marks that can be erased later.

Where a circle intersects a rhumb line, drill a ³⁄₁₆-inch hole ½ inch deep. There will be a total of 256 holes. A piece of tape folded around

Using Your
Traverse Board

*You can use your board in
exactly the same manner mariners
used them centuries ago. Here's
the drill:*

*Every half-hour, at the turn of
the half-hourglass, the helmsman
placed a peg in the hole of the
compass point that matched the
average direction the ship had been
steered during the last 30 minutes.
At the same time, the ship's speed
was taken on a chip log and a peg
was planted in the appropriate
hole on the speed grid.*

*The helmsman inserted the pegs
in a consistent order, starting at the
center of the rose and working outwards one row at a time, until the
eighth row of holes was reached at
the end of a four-hour watch.*

*Likewise, he placed the first
speed peg in the top row of the*
(continued on page 99)

your drill bit ½ inch from the tip will tell you when the bit reaches its
proper depth.

One inch below the bottom of the compass rose, draw two speed
grids measuring 2 inches by 4½ inches and filled with ½-inch squares.
Each vertical row of squares here represents one knot of ship's speed,

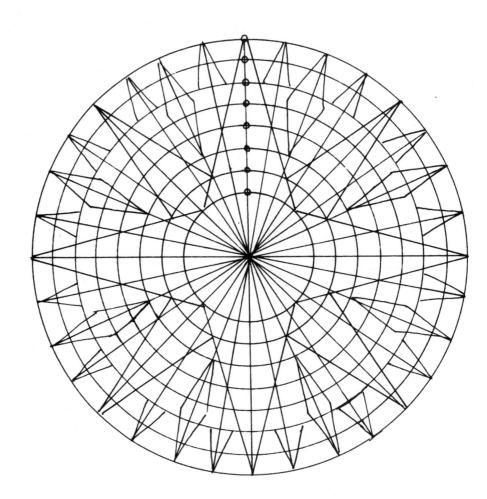

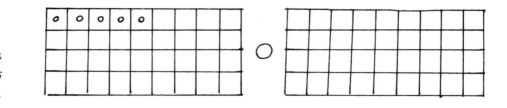

Figure 12-2
*Marking the points
of the compass.*

and this is sufficient for a maximum speed of 9 knots. If your boat goes faster than this, you'll need more squares.

Locate the exact center of each square and drill a ³⁄₁₆-inch hole ½ inch deep there. That's another 72 holes to drill.

Finally, drill two ½-inch holes ½ inch deep. One is at the center of the rose and the other is between the two grids—see Figure 12-1.

To complete the rose, pencil in the pattern shown in Figure 12-2, then paint the rose using a fine brush. If you fill in with solid color the outlines of the rhumb markers shown in Figure 12-1, you'll have a fine traverse board. When the paint is dry, erase the construction lines.

Ink the grid lines and inscribe the numerals along the top and the left side. You can repeat those numbrs down the right side, too, if you wish.

The numbers at the top are the ship's speed in knots; those on the left are the hours of the watch, broken into the first half-hour on the left grid, the second on the right, and so on. Erase any extra construction lines.

The peg holders are two pieces of ½-inch hardwood dowel cut 1 inch long. Glue them in the ½-inch holes and varnish the board. The pegs themselves are cut from the ³⁄₁₆-inch hardwood dowel. You'll need 16 pieces, each 1 inch long. You'll also need 16 pieces of string cut 8 inches long. Tie one end of each string to a small dowel or, if you have a surfeit of patience, drill a small hole in the face end of each dowel and glue the string in place. Tie the other end to the appropriate ½-inch peg.

You can break with tradition and do without the string altogether if you want—it's just to stop the pegs getting lost. Keep a small container for the dowels near the board. But if you take this short cut, you're honor-bound to admit that it's a departure from the classic instrument.

Your traverse board is now ready for display, or for use on your next voyage.

left-hand grid, the second peg in the top row of the right-hand grid, the third peg in the left-hand grid on the second row, and so on until the end of a four-hour watch.

With just a glance at the traverse board, a navigator could see what the ship's speed and direction had been during each half-hour increment of a four-hour watch. He could also quickly determine the ship's average speed and direction. In Figure 12-1, for example, the board shows a course of a fraction east of north and an average speed of 5½ knots.

These averages were chalked into a rough log, often just a hinged board that folded like a book, and the pegs were pulled out of the board for the next watch. When the information on the rough log was transferred into the smooth log and marked on the chart, the rough log was erased.

13 The Hand Lead

K NOWING THE DEPTH OF THE WATER under a vessel has always been a critical concern for mariners, especially those navigating narrow coastal waters with unmarked shoals or ship-wrecking ledges. And knowing the depth of the water can help you verify your position on a chart. That's why today's electronic depth finders are one of the most useful—and most used—pieces of equipment on a boat.

But like anything electronic, they can fail or give false readings at any time, so the cautious sailor always has a reliable backup. Nothing could more reliable than a lead (pronounced "led") line, which is just a gravity-powered lead weight attached to a line marked in fathoms.

Lead lines are probably the world's oldest navigational tools. Until the advent of electronic depthfinders, vessels in all waters and in all eras had lead lines aboard, and sailors who knew how to use them skillfully. Tales of ships' captains miraculously finding their way through fog and darkness with only a compass and lead are not just yarns. The old sailing instructions for the complicated and treacherous waters along the coast of England show clearly that navigators placed a tremendous emphasis on lead and line in their piloting.

Traditionally, there were two types of lead lines, both measuring in units of six feet, known as fathoms. The inshore version measured

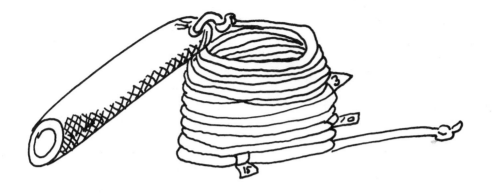

Figure 13-1
The hand lead.

down to 50 fathoms, and the deep-sea (pronounced "dipsey") lead for offshore work measured down to 200 fathoms. Knots and flags of various colors and materials were tied to the line to indicate fathoms by sight and feel. The different materials and configurations allowed the leadsman to find his depth even in utter darkness.

In addition, the old-fashioned lead had a hollow in its base to hold a dab of sticky tallow. This picked up bottom sediments that gave clues to the approximate location of the vessel. Modern charts still give bottom types. Furthermore, with practice it is often possible to tell whether you have struck mud or rock merely from the feeling in the line.

Making a Lead Line

Here's what you'll need:

- Lead pipe, OR 1¼"-diameter aluminum pipe with 4 to 7 lbs. of lead tire weights
- Light Dacron line, ¼" diameter. Length: 60' to 300', depending on depths in your cruising area

To make the hand lead, flatten one end of the lead pipe with a vise, and drill out a hole large enough to take your line. Tie the lead to the line with a bowline—see Figure 13-2. If your pipe isn't hefty enough, you can fill it with more lead. A weight of anywhere between 4 and 7 pounds is appropriate.

Figure 13-2
Four important knots. Clockwise, from top left: the bowline, overhand knot, figure-eight knot, and two half-hitches.

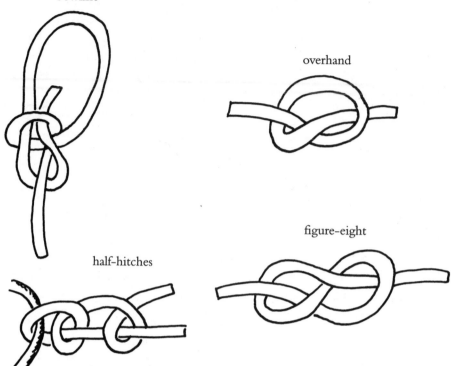

bowline

overhand

half-hitches

figure-eight

Figure 13-3
Heaving the lead.

If you can't find a lead pipe, pour melted lead into an aluminum pipe. (Melting and handling lead is discussed in Chapter 15.) There is no danger of melting the aluminum. Flatten and drill the end, as above.

You can mark each fathom of line with waterproof tape and write

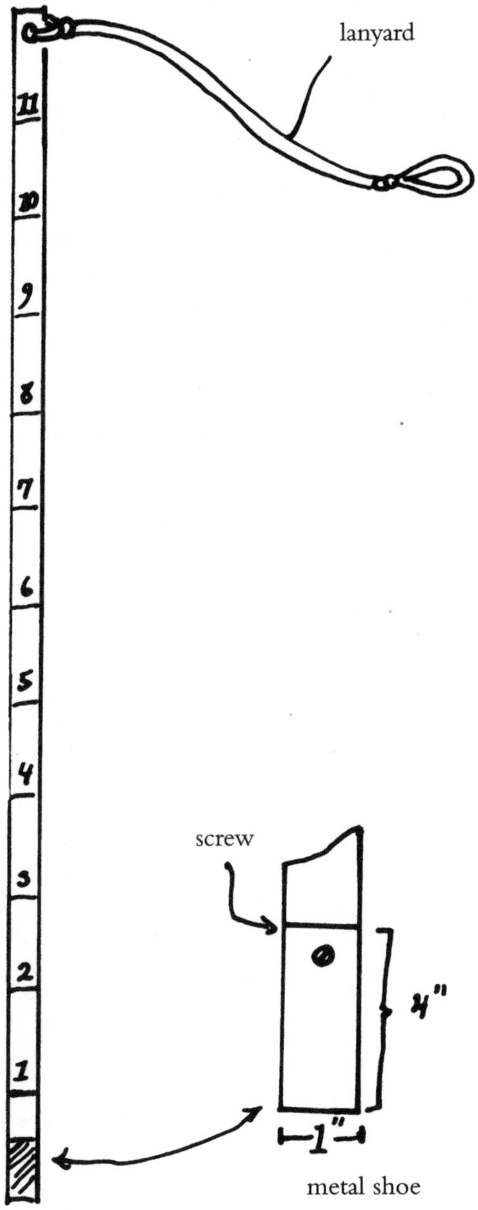

Figure 13-4
Sounding pole.

Using Your Lead Line

When you wish to take soundings, slow the boat until it almost stops. Soundings are always taken from the weather side. With a fairly light lead, you may be able to swing the lead overhand, like throwing a baseball, while standing on the foredeck.

With a heavier weight, the traditional way to cast the lead was for the leadsman to hold the loosely coiled line in one hand and to swing the lead on several feet of line with the other. He swung it fore and aft several times to gather momentum and then let it fly out ahead of the ship as far as it would go.

In either case, as the lead flies forward let go of the line and allow it to pay out through your fingers. When the line strikes bottom, you will feel a slight jolt. Immediately nip the line and read the depth where the line meets the water. The reading will seldom be exact in deep water because current and the line's weight cause the line to sag.

When navigating shallow areas with mud flats, narrow channels, or wildly varying tidal conditions, a sounding pole (Figure 13-4) can quickly and accurately show you where the deepest water lies. My pole is an inch or so in diameter and a dozen feet long, marked off in feet. I've used it to feel my way along channels only a few feet deep in water too cloudy to see bottom. Tie a lanyard through a hole in the top of the pole to keep from losing it.

the depth on the tape with waterproof marker. For the traditional manner of labeling a lead line, use the following markings:

Fathoms	Markings
2	2 strips of leather
3	3 strips of leather
5	white rag
7	red rag
10	leather with a hole in it
13	same as three
15	same as five
17	same as seven
20	2 knots
25	1 knot
30	3 knots
35	1 knot
40	4 knots

The Heaving Line

THE HEAVING LINE IS SIMPLE in concept and extremely useful in practice. It's just a light, ¼-inch line, 50 or so feet long, with a squarish, weighted knot called a monkey's fist at one end. Because of its light weight, a heaving line can be thrown farther than most other lines on board, so it's often used for passing mooring lines to the dock or other boats, or in an emergency, for getting a lifeline to someone in the water.

Old-time mariners used a lump of lead wrapped in a rag to weight their monkey's fists. A golf ball wrapped in a rag is an acceptable substitute and isn't as dangerous to catch. The fist itself is a decorative knot that can be used to adorn any number of projects. Here's how to tie a small fist with ¼-inch line.

monkey's fist

Figure 14-1
A heaving line.

heaving line

Figure 14-2
How to tie the monkey's fist knot.

Using Your Heaving Line

Heaving a line is one of those arts that gets better with practice. All too often, when a heaving line is needed, it's needed in an emergency. And all too often, there's a large crowd watching you make a mess of things.

Some sailors are able to grasp several coils of the line, with the weighted end one coil's-length away from the hand (at the bottom of the coil, in other words) and throw it overhand, elbow first. They start with a swing rearward, over the shoulder, and then let fly forward.

If you can get it right, there's little doubt that it's the strongest throw, and probably the most accurate. Most people, however, throw the line underhand and hope for the best. Some even try a sort of sideways swing and count themselves lucky if the line goes anywhere near its intended destination.

If you have a clear deck, and no lifelines for the line to catch on, or if you hang outside the rails, an underhand throw will send the line almost as far as an overhand throw would, especially if you make the coils a little larger than normal. The larger scope allows you to build up more momentum in the right direction before you are committed to letting go.

(continued on page 107)

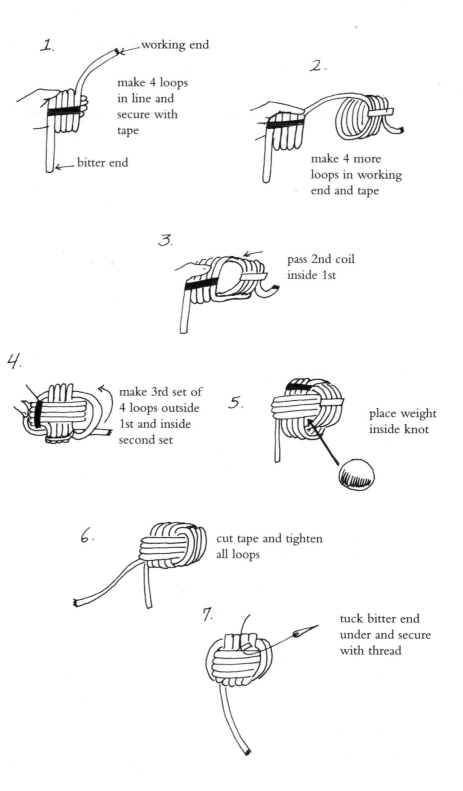

1. working end
make 4 loops in line and secure with tape
bitter end

2. make 4 more loops in working end and tape

3. pass 2nd coil inside 1st

4. make 3rd set of 4 loops outside 1st and inside second set

5. place weight inside knot

6. cut tape and tighten all loops

7. tuck bitter end under and secure with thread

Making a Heaving Line

Here's what you'll need:

- Nylon, polyester, or polypropylene line, ¼" diameter, 60' long
- One old golf ball and cloth rag

Tying a monkey's fist takes some practice, so don't worry if it takes you a few tries to succeed. Take one end of the line and make four loops around your hand. At the end of the fourth loop, bend the line to the right. See Figure 14-2. Then tape the loops together, remove your hand, and make four loops inside and at right angles to the previous four with the working end of the line. It takes a little dexterity to keep everything in place, so take it slowly. You can practice with three loops instead of four, if it suits you better.

Now pass the working end inside the second set of loops and outside and at right angles to the first set to make four more loops. Place the golf ball in the cavity at the center of the fist while it is still loose, then tighten the knot until the fist is firm and compact.

When the knot is tightened, you can cut the working end off short, whip it, and tuck it under the turns. Secure it there with needle and thread.

Generally, the coiled line is split in two, and one half is held in each hand. But if there is a fair lead from the deck, it often pays to let the second half run from there. First, make sure it's made fast to something on the boat. Then fake it down in large figure-eights, which will run free without kinking and fouling everything.

If you prefer to keep the second half in your hand, you might want to try a special coiling technique that ensures free running of the line. It's known as alternate hitch coiling. Ordinary, clockwise turns are alternated with hitches that impart twists in the other direction. These twists cancel each other out, allowing the line to run freely. This technique is fully explained in books on knots and ropework. If you opt to keep the second coil in your spare hand, make sure it's attached to your wrist. The longest, most accurate throw is worse than useless if the bitter end goes flying off with the coils.

If you have a choice, heave with the wind. If you're forced to heave against the wind, try to keep the line low. When you're heaving across the wind, aim upwind a bit. And try not to hit the gawkers on the jetty, tempting as it might be. A clout from a golf ball can be very painful, even if it is covered with rope.

Figure 14-3
Heaving a line.

A simple Turk's head knot, followed around two or three times, and capsized into a sphere, also makes a good knot for the end of a heaving line. Both ends can be worked tightly into the knot, so you can form a closed bight, or loop, of several inches, that allows the weighted knot to be attached to any number of different lines.

Incidentally, the nylon line is strongest and stretchiest. Polyester (Dacron) is slightly weaker, but stretches very little. Polypropylene doesn't last as long but compensates by floating, so that lines that land in a heap three feet away in the water don't foul the propeller.

The Chip Log

THE SIMPLEST OF ALL SPEED-MEASURING devices is the Dutchman's log—a piece of wood or balled-up paper thrown overboard at the bow of the vessel. By counting the seconds it takes the boat to leave this "log" astern, a sailor can easily compute a vessel's progress using this formula: Speed (in knots) equals .60 times boat length (in feet) divided by time (in seconds).

For example, if a 20-foot long boat takes five seconds to pass a log, its speed is .60 multiplied by 20, divided by 5, which equals 2.4 knots. The constant .60 approximates the number of seconds in an hour (3,600) divided by the number of feet in a nautical mile (6,076).

Another way to measure speed requires marks along the boat's rail at intervals of 1.688 feet (1 foot 8¼ inches). Since 1.688 feet per second is one knot, you can determine your speed by dividing the number of marks that pass the log by the number of seconds it takes for them to pass. If the log passes five marks in three seconds, for instance, then dividing five by three gives you 1.7 knots.

The chip log works on the same basic principle as the Dutchman's log, but is much more accurate. It is simply a pie-shaped wooden plank fastened to a line knotted at regular intervals. Traditional chip logs used a line of light cotton, such as ⅛-inch-diameter codline.

Figure 15-1
The chip log.

The first chip logs were developed in the 1500s. Before that, seamen made educated guesses to gauge speed, using such clues as seaweed passing by the hull or size of the wake. An experienced navigator could usually estimate a ship's speed to within a knot, but even Columbus consistently underestimated his speed on his first voyage.

The chip log is still a very accurate way to measure speed, and is without question the most reliable method. For all their convenience, knotmeters—and even the revolving spinners of taffrail logs—easily clog with weed and debris. Also, through-hull knotmeters can leak or break off, with troublesome consequences.

The one drawback of the chip log is that for ease of working it requires two people: one to throw the log and handle the line, the other to read the stopwatch or sandglass. However, with a bit of practice and preparation, you can do it alone.

Figure 15-2
Heaving the log.

Making a Chip Log

Here's what you'll need:

- One piece waterproof plywood, ½" × 16" × 21"
- Scrap lead, 5 oz.
- Four copper tacks, ½" long
- One hardwood dowel or peg, ½" × 3"
- One hardwood dowel, ¾" × 24"
- 3⁄16" line (length varies—see formula below)

On the plywood, draw two 5-inch circles for the log line reel-ends and an equilateral triangle 10 inches on a side for the chip. Scribe the curve of the lower edge of the chip with a compass set at 10 inches and placed on the apex of the triangle. Cut out the chip and the circles with a sabersaw. Then drill a 3⁄16-inch hole 1 inch from each lower corner of the chip and a 3⁄16-inch hole near the chip's apex. Also, drill a ¾-inch hole in the center of each reel end.

The chip is weighted so it will float upright, perpendicular to the water's surface. There are two ways to weight the chip. The traditional approach involves pouring lead into a hole near the bottom of the chip,

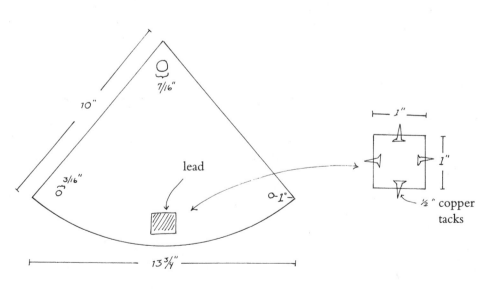

Figure 15-3
Details of the chip.

but if you don't want to work with hot lead, you can drill and screw a few tire weights to the bottom edge of the chip.

To make a chip with a traditional look (Figure 15-3) cut a 1" × 1" hole halfway between the two lower holes and close to the chip's lower edge. Drive four copper tacks halfway into the sides of the hole. The part of the tack that projects into the hole will hold the lead in place.

Clamp a metal or wooden plate tightly to one side of the chip to prevent the molten lead from running out. Lay the chip flat with the open side of the hole face up. Your "mold" is now ready for the hot lead.

Lead melts readily, so your "furnace" needn't be elaborate. I use a backyard barbecue grill. Put the lead in a coffee can and pile a small amount of burning charcoal around it. In about 20 minutes, after the lead melts, pick up the can with fireplace tongs and pour the lead into the hole in the chip until it is just brimming. There will be some slag on the top, but this will stay in the can as you pour.

Even when working with this small amount of lead, you need to take certain precautions. Be sure to wear gloves and safety glasses throughout this operation, and to work carefully to avoid burns from the hot metal. Keep everything dry. A small drop of water can cause spectacular and dangerous splattering. Also, always melt lead outdoors where there's less danger of anybody's breathing lead fumes. Stay inside while the lead is melting and wear a respirator or hold your breath when it's time to pour.

While the lead is still molten, press another small wood or metal plate over the chip to flatten the lead and press it evenly into the hole. The lead will set and cool within 10 minutes. Seal the chip with several coats of epoxy, then paint or varnish.

How much 3/16-inch line you'll need depends on the timing interval you choose and how fast your boat can go.

The formula for spacing knots on a log line, in feet, is 1.688 times the timing interval in seconds. Thus, a timing interval of 10 seconds, for example, would require knots 16.88 feet—16 feet 10½ inches— apart. Try this to start with.

Assuming your boat doesn't plane, your boat's hull speed—its theoretical maximum speed—is the square root of your vessel's waterline

Using Your Chip Log

First, tap the wooden peg lightly into the top hole. Then, while holding one end of the reel in one hand, heave the chip over the stern clear of the wake. When the chip is tossed over the taffrail (at the stern), it essentially stops dead in the water and pulls the knotted log line off a reel as the vessel proceeds along its course.

Let the line pay out smoothly from the reel and begin timing when the rag passes over the rail. The rag marks the beginning of the timing period; the 20-foot interval allows you to heave the log beyond the boat's turbulent wake before the clock starts.

Let's presume you've chosen to space your knots at intervals of 16 feet 10½ inches (see formula above). This means your measuring time will always be exactly 10 seconds.

Count the knots as they pass over the rail. At the end of 10 seconds give the line a sharp tug to free the peg. The chip will then lie flat, making it easier to rewind the line. Keep your fingers clamped on

(continued on page 113)

LATITUDE HOOKS AND AZIMUTH RINGS

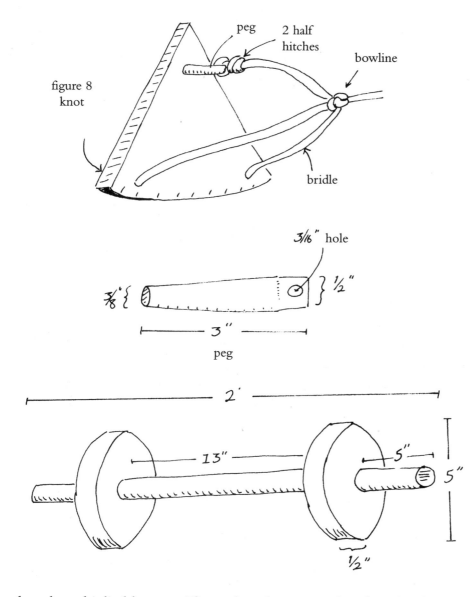

Figure 15-4
The bridle and the reel.

peg

2 half hitches

bowline

figure 8 knot

bridle

3/16" hole

1/2"

3/8"

3"

peg

2'

13"

5"

5"

1/2"

the line, and re-count the number of knots as you wind the line in, just to check.

The number of knots indicates the speed, hence the origin of the term "knot" as a speed of one nautical mile per hour, and the phrase "She's logging 10 knots." Commonly, the log was read at the beginning of a new watch, or whenever the ship changed speed.

Experiment with the knot spacing, the time interval, and the length of line, which are all related according to the formula above.

In days gone past, ship's log lines often had knots spaced at intervals of 47 feet 3 inches, which was the length that would run out in 28 seconds at a speed of one knot. Speed was therefore gauged by the number of knots that ran out in 28 seconds as shown by a special time-glass, later superseded by a watch with a second hand.

This greater knot interval gives a slightly more accurate reading, but it requires an impractical amount of line for small yachts— almost three times as much line as that required for the 16-foot 10½-inch interval suggested above.

length multiplied by 1.34. If your boat has a waterline length of about 17 feet, for instance, it will be hard pressed ever to exceed 5.53 knots. Round up to the nearest knot, say 6 knots, multiply hull speed by the length between knots on the line—6 times 16.88 feet—and add another 25 feet for "stray line" to clear the wake, as well as the extra amount taken up by the knots themselves and the bridle.

In this instance, a line 125 feet long should be just about right. If you can't find line long enough, you can splice or knot two lengths together or shorten the timing interval. If you choose to join two or more lines with a knot, place the knot where a normal timing knot would be.

A special three-line bridle keeps the chip square to the log line while measuring speed and then releases one corner when it's time to retrieve the line. See Figure 15-4. First, cut a 30-inch length off the log line and tie a loose bowline (Chapter 13, Figure 13-2) in the log line's new end. Leave a 12-inch length of the working end protruding from the knot.

Pass the 30-inch piece of line halfway through the bowline's loop, then cinch the knot tight. Push the ends of this short line through the chip's lower holes and secure them on the far side of the chip with figure-eight knots so the bowline is centered between the holes.

Next, whittle one end of the ½-inch dowel so it tapers gently to a ⅜-inch diameter at its tip (Figure 15-4). Drill a ³⁄₁₆-inch hole through the widest end of the dowel. Find the protruding end of the bowline and push it through this hole. Bring the end of the line back to the standing part and make two-half hitches to secure the peg temporarily. Finally, lightly tap the peg into the top hole of the chip and adjust the length of its line with the half-hitches so the chip is horizontal when hanging down freely from its bridle. The bridle is now complete.

Tie a small rag in the line 20 feet from the chip. Measuring from the rag, tie overhand knots in the line at the appropriate spots, using the formula mentioned above.

Figure 15-5
An improved reel.

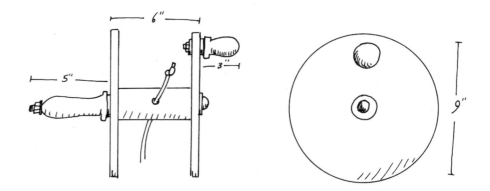

To hold the line, you'll need a log reel. The simplest reel can be made from a ¾-inch dowel and the two 5-inch plywood disks you cut out earlier. Glue each disk 5 inches from the ends of the dowel with epoxy or waterproof glue, then sand; stain, varnish, or paint.

A more complex reel is shown in Figure 15-5. This device works like a fishing reel and makes rewinding the line easier and faster.

16 The Weatherglass

THIS CRUDE TYPE OF BAROMETER was first made in Holland in the 16th century and remained in common use until the last century. The classic weatherglass is a pitcher-shaped object of blown-glass partially filled with clear or colored water. A narrow, upturned tube leads from the bottom of the glass to a point just above the water level. Because the tube is the only opening in the glass, the water effectively seals the air in the reservoir from the outside. Changes in the atmospheric pressure compress or expand the trapped air and push the water up or down the tube.

Making a Weatherglass

Here's what you'll need:

- One 12-oz. bottle
- One cork or rubber stopper
- Copper tubing, ¼" diameter, 2" long.
- Clear plastic tubing, ⅜" diameter, 12" long
- Copper or brass wire, 12" long
- Cotton string, 16 feet long

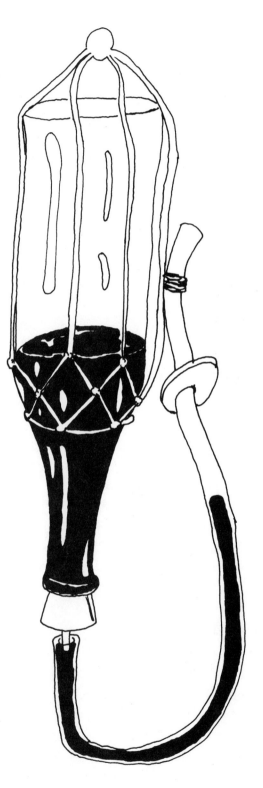

Figure 16-1
The weatherglass.

Figure 16-2
How the water level varies in the tube with high atmospheric pressure (left) and low pressure (right).

H   L

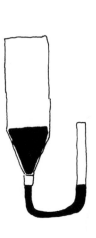

Using Your Weatherglass

Forecasting the weather with a barometer or weatherglass is mostly a matter of practice and experience. It must be read frequently because it is the rate and direction of movement that are important.

You might like to graduate your barometer by marking the positions of the water level in the tube.

In the middle latitudes, a high barometer reads about 30.50 inches (1,033 millibars). A low barometer reads 29.50 inches (999 millibars.) The average reading at sea level is 29.90 inches (1,013 millibars).

If you record your readings every four or six hours, and plot the results on graph paper, you'll have a good picture of whether the air pressure is rising or falling, and—most important—how quickly it's changing.

(continued on page 119)

This weatherglass has the virtues of being inexpensive and maintenance-free. If you wish, you can take it aboard a small craft as an auxiliary to the aneroid barometer that should be aboard any cruising boat. An antique bottle makes an attractive reservoir, though I've made weatherglasses out of brown beer bottles that work quite well.

Find a cork that fits tightly into the bottle's neck, put the cork in a vise, and gently drill a ¼-inch hole through it. You can also find pre-drilled rubber stoppers at hobby shops, hardware stores, and home-brewing suppliers. Smear a little epoxy on the copper tubing and push it though the hole in the cork. Then press the clear plastic tubing over the end of the copper tube.

Slip a rubber washer with a ⅜-inch interior diameter over the plastic tube. The washer marks the water level in the tube at the last

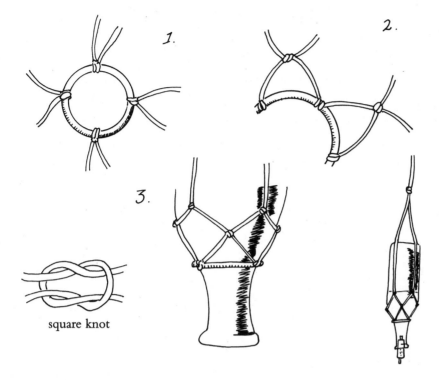

1.

2.

3.

square knot

Figure 16-3
Making the bridle.

observation so you can see how much and in what direction the water has moved.

A weatherglass has to remain level for comparative readings. You can make a simple string bridle that will allow it to hang straight from a hook. See Figure 16-3.

First, fashion a collar out of a piece of brass or copper wire that fits loosely around the neck of the bottle. Then take four pieces of cotton string about 4 feet long. Double them, and pass the ends through the center loop around the ring. Arrange the tightened loops evenly around the collar as shown and tie one line from each pair to a line from an adjacent pair using a square knot.

Make sure the strings leading to each knot are the same length. Repeat this step to make another set of knots. Now, gather up the free

Remember that water rising in the tube is an indication of decreasing pressure—what is usually referred to as a falling barometer.

Here's how to interpret the results:

***Steady, persistent decrease in pressure:** The sign of an approaching depression. There's bad weather coming. But often the strongest wind won't come until the pressure starts to rise again.*

***Steady, persistent increase in pressure:** The weather will remain the same as it is now for some time to come.*

***No change in pressure:** Fair weather will continue.*

***Sudden rise, or sudden fall, in pressure:** Unsettled weather is on the way. Gales accompanied by a rise in pressure are usually more gusty and cantankerous than gales that arrive on a falling barometer.*

THE WEATHERGLASS **119**

ends of the bridle and tie them together at a point a little more than a bottle's length from the collar. Cut off any excess.

With a short piece of wire, attach the end of the tube to the bridle at a spot above the water level in the bottle; make sure the tube isn't pinched anywhere. Finally, pour about a cup of water in the bottle, bung the cork and tubes into its mouth, and hang your glass from the bridle in some convenient location.

The Pelorus

CHAPTER 17

THE PELORUS, A HUMBLE LITTLE DEVICE for taking relative bearings, is today little understood, and seldom used—although it is available from marine stores and marine catalogs—because its function has largely been taken over by the hand bearing compass. This is a pity, because the pelorus is useful and accurate. There should be one aboard every boat.

The pelorus consists of a base and a pair of sights on a pointer that rotates above a 360-degree compass rose mounted on a disk that also rotates. The device is also referred to as a dumb compass because it has no magnets and cannot on its own give a bearing you can plot on a chart.

Using a pelorus isn't difficult, yet most sailors prefer a hand bearing compass, for understandable reasons. Most hand-held compasses are compact enough to fit in a pocket or hang around a neck. They require no math, and one person—even the helmsman—can take a bearing without assistance. Yet while a hand bearing compass is convenient, its bearings might sometimes be suspect. That's because, in theory, its magnets are affected by ferrous metal (such as an engine) and electromagnetic influences generated in electrical wiring and electronic instruments.

Figure 17-1
The pelorus.

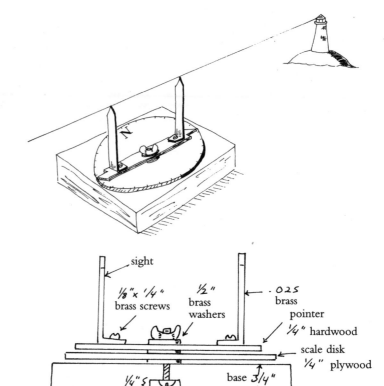

Figure 17-2
Plan and side views of the finished pelorus.

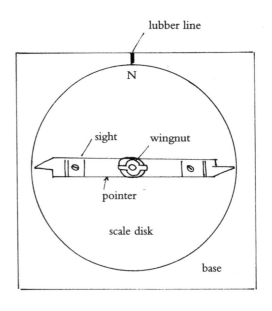

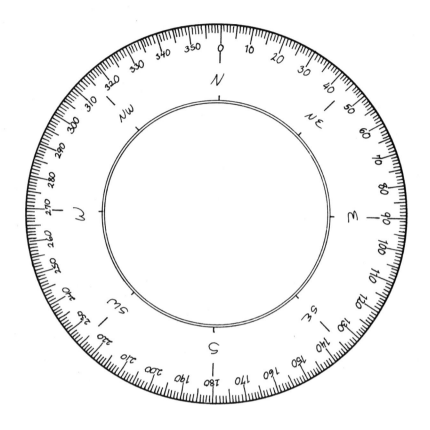

Figure 17-3
A pelorus card.

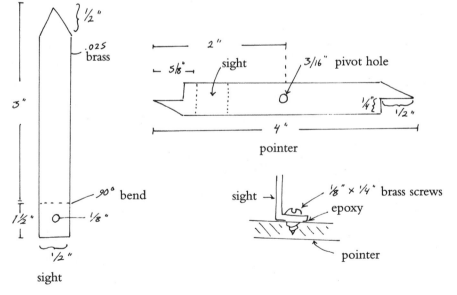

sight

pointer

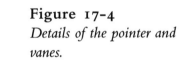

sight

pointer

Figure 17-4
Details of the pointer and vanes.

Using Your Pelorus

Taking a bearing with a pelorus is simple. First, position the base so the lubber line points forward and is parallel to the boat's centerline. Then rotate the scale disk so that 0 degrees points forward. Now while the helmsman steers as steady a course as possible, line up the sights on the pelorus with a landmark, calling "Mark" when the sight is taken and tightening the wingnut to keep the pointer from moving. The helmsman then reports the compass heading, and you read the angle on the pelorus, known as a relative bearing. The relative bearing added to the compass heading gives the compass bearing of the landmark.

Say, for example, your boat's heading by the steering compass is 030 degrees and a pelorus sight on a buoy to starboard reads 045 degrees. Adding 045 to 030 gives you the compass bearing of the buoy—075 degrees. See Figure 17-5. Of course, you could get the same reading by sighting over the steering compass. Indeed, many ship's compasses were fitted with an azimuth ring and sights for the purpose of taking bearings. But a boat's main compass is often installed in a bulkhead or set flush into the deck, which makes it impossible to use for bearings, unless you pause and deliberately point the ship's head at the buoy or other object.
(continued on page 125)

In practice, however, it's usually not difficult to find a spot on the deck of a pleasureboat, or in the cockpit, where the compass is out of range of magnetic deviation. It is also very easy to check the accuracy of a hand bearing compass by taking a bearing of the sun at sunrise or sunset, or by comparing its reading with that of a charted compass range.

While a good hand bearing compass costs a lot of money (a cheap one is worthless), you can build a pelorus for a few dollars, at most, and get accurate bearings every time by comparing its readings with those from your standard steering compass.

You can also employ a pelorus (or sun compass, Chapter 18) to make an accurate deviation table for your compass, to find the azimuth of the sun and other bodies for celestial navigation, or to take the relative bearings of other craft.

As with any instrument, precision is important. Measure accurately, take your time, and your pelorus will serve you faithfully.

Making a Pelorus

Here's what you'll need:

- One piece hardwood or plywood, ¾" × 5" × 5"
- Four cork pads
- One piece plywood, ¼" × 4" × 4"
- One roundhead brass bolt with washer and wingnut, ³⁄₁₆" × 1½"
- One sheet .025" brass, 2" × 4"
- Three brass washers, ½" diameter with ³⁄₁₆" hole
- One piece hardwood, ¼" × ½" × 4"
- Two brass screws, ⅛" × ¼"

Take the 5-inch-square base and draw a light diagonal line connecting each corner. Draw the lubber line in permanent ink from the point where the diagonals intersect—the exact center of the base—to the midpoint of one side of the base.

Drill a ³⁄₁₆-inch hole through the center of the base, then on the underside of the base, drill a larger hole, a countersink just wide enough and deep enough to accept the head of the bolt. See Figure 17-2. Stain and varnish the base and glue cork pads to its underside to prevent slipping.

The 4-inch-diameter scale disk is made from the ¼-inch plywood. To make a perfectly round disk with a scrollsaw or bandsaw, first draw two diagonals from each corner of the plywood and drill a ³⁄₁₆-inch hole where they intersect. Then, through this center hole, bolt the plywood to a piece of scrap so the plywood overhangs the scrap and can turn freely without any side-to-side or up-and-down wobble. Clamp the scrap to the saw's table top so the blade just touches the midpoint of the plywood's edge. By slowly rotating the plywood past the moving saw blade, you'll cut a perfect 4-inch circle with no guesswork about finding its center.

When the sum of the relative bearing and the compass angle is 360 or greater, subtract 360 from the total to arrive at an understandable bearing. For instance, if your boat is sailing due east (90 degrees) and the object you sight bears 270 degrees by the pelorus, relative to the ship's head, then adding 90 to 270 gives 360, or 0. So the object is bearing due north.

Likewise, if you are sailing southwest at 215 degrees and the landmark bears 325 degrees by pelorus, adding the two together gives 540 degrees. Subtract 360 and you get a bearing of 180 degrees—due south.

Another method for taking bearings with the pelorus is to turn the scale disk until it matches the compass heading. This way, compass bearings can be read directly off the scale after a sight is taken. The problem then is that the helmsman has the difficult task of holding a perfectly straight course while the sight is taken. As before, when you correct for deviation, do so only for the compass heading of the boat, not for the bearing.

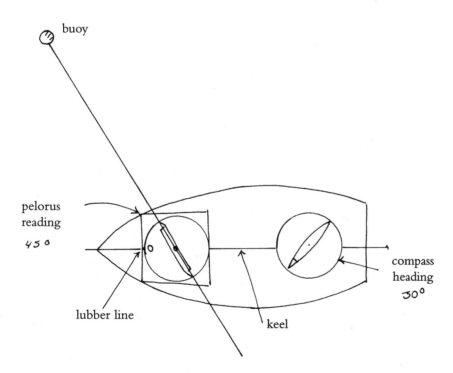

Figure 17-5
Taking a bearing with a pelorus.

You can photocopy and cut out the scale in Figure 17-3, or use a compass rose from an old chart or plotting sheet. Mount the scale on the 4-inch scale disk with Elmer's Glue-All and protect it with two or three coats of shellac.

Fashion the pointer out of a piece of ¼-inch hardwood such as teak, and drill a ³⁄₁₆-inch hole in its exact center. Any imprecision here will undermine the accuracy of the instrument.

Cut the sight vanes out of .025-inch sheet brass following the pattern shown in Figure 17-4. Drill a ⅛-inch mounting hole ¼ inch from the square end of each vane, and bend a 90-degree flange 1½ inch from the same ends. Fasten the vanes ⅝ inch from the ends of the pointer with the 1¼-inch brass screws and epoxy; make sure they are set perfectly square to the pointer. Now you can assemble all the pieces as shown in Figure 17-2.

The Sun Compass

THE SUN COMPASS IS A SIMPLE TOOL that uses the sun to determine compass deviation caused by magnetic influences aboard a vessel. It is nothing more than a compass card with a tall shadow pin set square in its center. This device is employed by professional compass adjusters in their work.

In the 1800s, ship's compasses often had built-in shadow pins to check for compass error. The sun's azimuth could be found exactly by calculation, which meant that compass deviation and variation could easily be established. Once deviation had been determined by swinging ship (see below), subsequent compass deflections were therefore the result of variation, the amount a compass was deflected from true north in a particular region or locale.

A sun compass can also be used to take bearings of the sun, to find the sun's azimuth, and to find a ship's true course, free of variation and deviation.

Figure 18-1
The sun compass.

Using Your Sun
Compass
The best time to swing ship
with a sun compass is in the
morning or afternoon when the
sun's shadow is longer, and if
possible, on a calm day with a
flat sea.
Place the sun compass in a
convenient spot on deck, clear
of any shade, near the ship's
compass. Steer the boat north
by the compass and rotate the
base until the sun's shadow
falls on the 0-degree mark.
Now turn the boat so the
sun-compass shadow falls at
180 degrees. Now read your
steering compass. If it also reads
180, there is no deviation on
north-south headings. If there is
a difference, remove half the
difference between your compass
heading and 180 using your
compass's N-S compensator
screw (and a non-magnetic
screwdriver). Now turn the boat
until the sun compass reads 15
degrees. If the ship's compass
reads 015 degrees, there is no
deviation on that heading. If
the ship's compass reads 016,
the deviation is one degree
(continued on page 129)

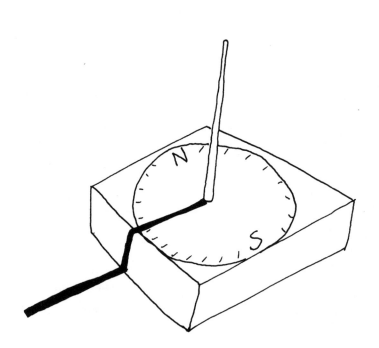

Making a Sun Compass

Here's what you'll need:

- One piece of plywood or hardwood, ½" × 5" × 5"
- One 22-gauge brass wire, 4" long
- Four rubber or cork pads

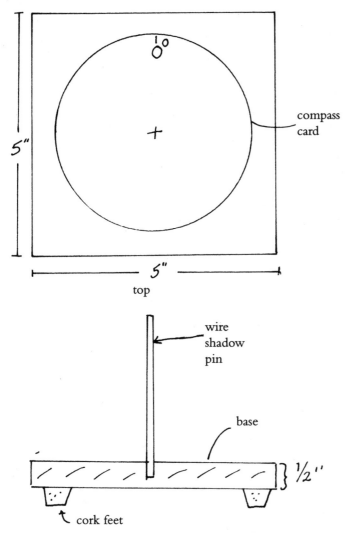

top

side

wire shadow pin

base

compass card

½"

cork feet

Figure 18-2
*Details of sun compass
construction.*

westerly. Remove half the
deviation again. *For instance,
if the steering compass reads
190 degrees, then the deviation
on that heading is 10 degrees
westerly.*

*Every 15 degrees, follow the
same procedure, turning the base
so the shadow matches your
heading, then noting where the
shadow falls on the compass
when you turn to the reciprocal
course.*

*Any deviation you find
applies to the reciprocal heading. And be aware that the sun
keeps moving—about one
degree every four minutes—so
you shouldn't run very far in
any one direction. Following
this procedure, you should be
able to remove nearly all deviation from a compass. If not,
you can make up a deviation
table.*

*As with the pelorus (Chap-
ter 17), record your results on a
deviation graph to check for
anomalous readings, then
mount a deviation curve or
table near your compass. After
that, you won't have to worry
about your compass steering
you wrong in fog or at night.*

Drill a ³⁄₃₂-inch hole in the center of the plywood base for the wire
pointer, sand the base smooth, then apply a couple of coats of varnish.
Small rubber or cork pads glued to the bottom of the base will prevent
skidding.

You can photocopy and cut out the compass card in Figure 17-3
on page 123, or use the compass rose from a chart. Place the center of
the card over the center of the base and align the 0-degree mark as

THE SUN COMPASS **129**

shown. Glue the card to the base with Elmer's Glue-All and cover with several coats of shellac.

Glue the brass-wire shadow pin into the center hole with epoxy and make sure it is absolutely straight and perpendicular to the base.

Because the sun compass must be level to work accurately, you may also want to attach a small spirit level to the base or card.

The Octant

THE FIRST DOUBLE-REFLECTING INSTRUMENTS—the forerunners of modern-day sextants—were invented nearly simultaneously in England and America in 1731. The American inventor, Thomas Godfrey, was an associate of Benjamin Franklin. John Hadley, a London instrument maker and member of the prestigious Royal Society, created the English device. Oddly enough, Sir Isaac Newton had invented a similar instrument some 30 years earlier, but had never publicized it. Hadley's device quickly became the more popular and its use spread rapidly, although many tradition-bound officers still clung to their mirror backstaffs (Chapter 10).

Basically, double-reflecting instruments use two mirrors to bring a celestial body's reflection down level with the horizon. An index mirror mounted on a pivoting index arm reflects the image of a celestial body onto a fixed horizon mirror. Half of the vertically split horizon mirror is silvered to bounce the reflection from the index mirror back to the eye; the other half is clear so the horizon can be sighted. A navigator rotates the index arm until the reflection in the horizon mirror appears to touch or split the horizon, then reads the angular altitude of the body off the arc on the instrument's limb. Because the horizon and the reflection are on the same sight line, ocular parallax—the problem that plagued such devices as the cross-staff—is eliminated.

The principle at work in a double-reflecting instrument is simple: The angle of incidence always equals the angle of reflection. In other words, when you see an object in a mirror, the angle that object makes with the mirror equals the angle the mirror makes with you. If two mirrors are held parallel and facing one another, the same is true; the angles of incidence and reflection remain equal.

Figure 19-1
The octant.

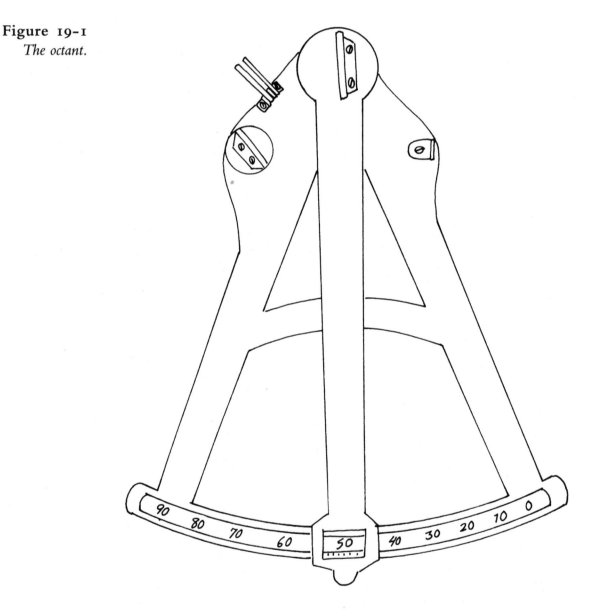

But if the mirrors are not parallel, as is the case with a double-reflecting instrument, then the angle of the second reflection (from the face of the horizon mirror to the eye) is double the original angle of incidence (from the face of the index mirror to the body being sighted). For this reason, each degree on the instrument's arc scale is actually laid out in half-degree increments.

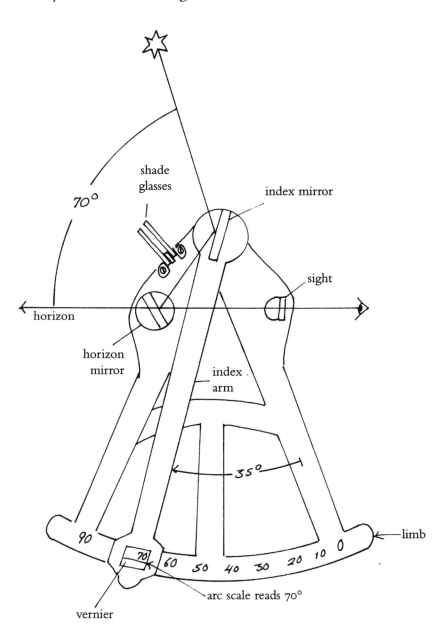

Figure 19-2
The parts of the vernier octant.

Using Your Octant: A
Pole Star Sight

To enjoy using your octant,
you'll need a current nautical
almanac and a watch or clock set to
Greenwich Mean Time (GMT)—
also known as Universal Coordi-
nated Time. You can buy an almanac
from any nautical chart agent or
marine store. And the watch doesn't
have to be a chronometer. Knowing
the time to the nearest minute is
good enough to start you off on two
simple sights.
The first is the Pole Star sight.
You need to be able to see both
Polaris and the horizon, of course,
so you're usually limited to twi-
light at dawn or dusk. This period
lasts only about 20 minutes; you
won't need your shade glasses.
Face the horizon and move the
index arm toward you until the
real and reflected horizons coin-
cide. Then with both eyes open,
raise the sextant and sight directly
on Polaris. You should see both the
real star and its reflected image in
the horizon mirror. Now, as you
slowly lower the sextant to sight
the horizon again, push the index
arm away from you so the star's
reflection stays in the center of the
mirror. This takes practice. When
(continued on page 135)

The first practical, double-reflecting instruments for navigation were called octants because their arcs spanned one-eighth of a circle: 45 degrees. But because of their double-reflecting mirrors, octants could actually measure angles up to 90 degrees and so were frequently and confusingly called quadrants (Chapter 5). Octants were normally built of ebony or rosewood with a brass arc and other fittings. In rare cases, the arc was of ivory or silver.

The true sextant, so named because its arc covers one-sixth of a circle (60 degrees), was invented late in the 18th century. The arc of the first sextants read up to 120 degrees; modern sextants now usually go farther than that. Early sextants had a vernier scale on the index arm for more precise reading of angles; modern instruments have a micrometer drum for the same purpose. Sextants today also usually have shade glasses to reduce glare when sighting the sun, as well as a telescope eyepiece to improve the accuracy of star sights. Both sextant and octant coexisted until the second half of the 19th century, when the sextant, with its ability to measure a wider range of angles, became the navigator's instrument of choice. Now the term sextant encompasses any double-reflecting instrument, regardless of the size of its arc.

Making an Octant

Here's what you'll need:

- One piece of hardwood plywood, or a mahogany plank, ½" × 11" × 12½"
- One piece .025" sheet brass, 2" × 6"
- One piece .005" sheet brass, 1" × 2¼"
- One plank hardwood, ¼" × 4" × 13"
- Six ⅛" roundhead brass screws, ⅜" long
- Two ³⁄₁₆" slotted flathead brass bolts, 1" long, with brass washers and locknuts
- One ⅛" slotted brass bolt, ¾" long, with locknut and ¼"-diameter brass washer
- Two mirrors, 1" × 1" and 1" × 1½"

This is by far the most complex project in the book, and requires a healthy investment in time and effort to complete. It is also a rewarding undertaking, and when you have finished you will possess a handsome and useful tool that can be used as a learner's sextant for celestial navigation, coastal piloting, or display.

This project is modeled on a rosewood octant of 1783. The materials list is not extensive or expensive, and you can probably build the

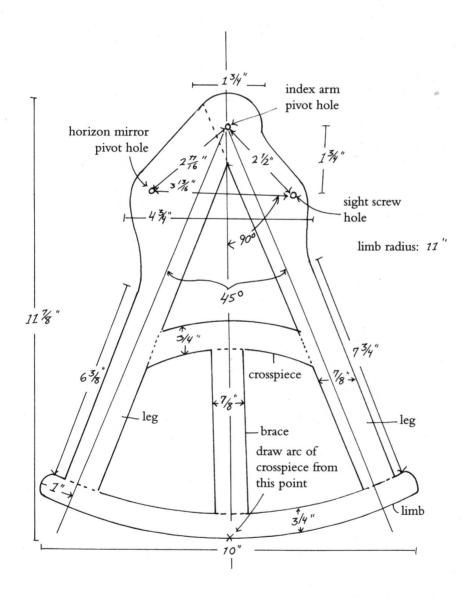

you've sighted the horizon, adjust the index arm so the reflected image of the star appears to touch the horizon.

If Polaris were absolutely directly over the North Pole, its true altitude would equal your latitude. But the Pole Star can veer just over 2 degrees east or west of the pole.

This doesn't matter much if you're happy to be within a degree or two of the correct figure. But if you want greater precision, you'll need to apply a correction to the sight. You'll find it in a table in your almanac, together with other corrections for dip (the height of your eye above sea level), and refraction (deflection of the star's rays by the atmosphere). You will already have corrected your observed altitude by adding or subtracting the index error of your instrument. That, together with the dip and refraction corrections, turns your observed altitude into a true altitude—from which you add or subtract the amount given for the Pole Star's wanderings.

The result—your latitude—can be converted into nautical miles north or south of the equator. Each degree equals 60 nautical miles and each minute equals 1 nautical mile.

Figure 19-3
The layout of the frame

basic model for considerably less than the average monthly household telephone bill, or about what you'd pay for a plastic practice sextant. Don't skimp on the plywood for the frame. Pick out the best sheet you can and look it over carefully for any imperfections before buying it. A one-piece plywood frame simplifies construction, but you can also

Figure 19-4
Details of the index arm.

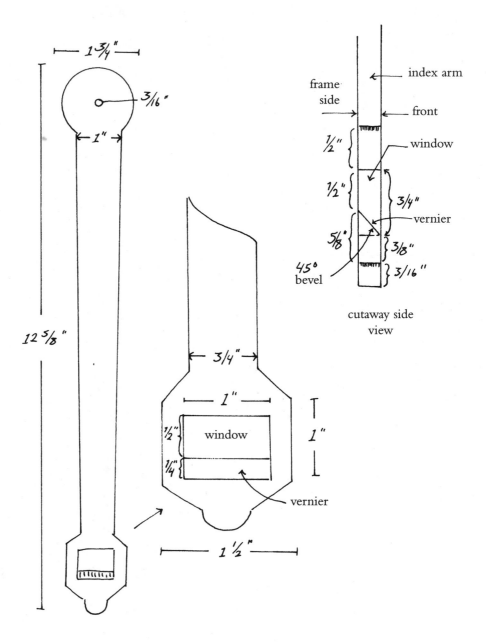

make your frame with hardwood pieces held together with mortise-and-tenon joints, just as the early instrument makers did. Rosewood, a tropical wood often used in instrument making, is fairly easy to work and is not excessively expensive in the small amounts you need. Mahogany is another option. The dashed lines in Figure 19-3 show the locations of the joints

The Body of the Octant

Before you mark up your wood, first make a full-scale drawing of the frame. Draw the limb with a batten or one-armed protractor pinned ⅜ inch below the top center of the frame. This marks the pivot point for the index arm. A folded piece of tape with a small hole poked in it will hold the tip of the pen on the batten or protractor.

Draw the index arm pattern as well (Figure 19-4) and make sure it fits the frame. On the index arm, there is a small window with an inward-beveled "sill" where the vernier is attached. Cutting this window and bevel is probably best accomplished with wood knives. Finish with a file and then with sandpaper glued to a small block.

To save you the painstaking task of drawing your own arc scale and vernier, a full-sized arc and vernier are provided in Figures 19-5 and 19-6. Photocopy them at a good copy center on their best bond paper. I recommend an off-white or ivory stock. Make several copies in case of errors or imperfections, and spray on an artist's fixative to prevent smudging. With fine scissors or an X-Acto knife, carefully cut out the arc and vernier. Place the arc scale on the limb in your pattern so that the bottom of the scale is ⅛ inch from the bottom of the limb and its 0-, 45-, and 90-degree marks align exactly with the lines in Figure 19-3 that radiate from the pivot point of the index arm.

When you are satisfied that the patterns match up properly, transfer the frame pattern to the ½-inch board and the index-arm pattern to the ¼-inch board with carbon paper. Carefully cut them out with a scroll saw. Just to be safe, take some practice cuts to get a feel for cutting these curves before you attack the frame.

Now make a disk on which to mount the horizon mirror. Take

Figure 19-5
The degree scale of the arc.

Figure 19-6
The vernier scale.

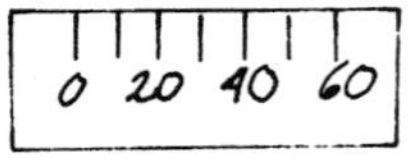

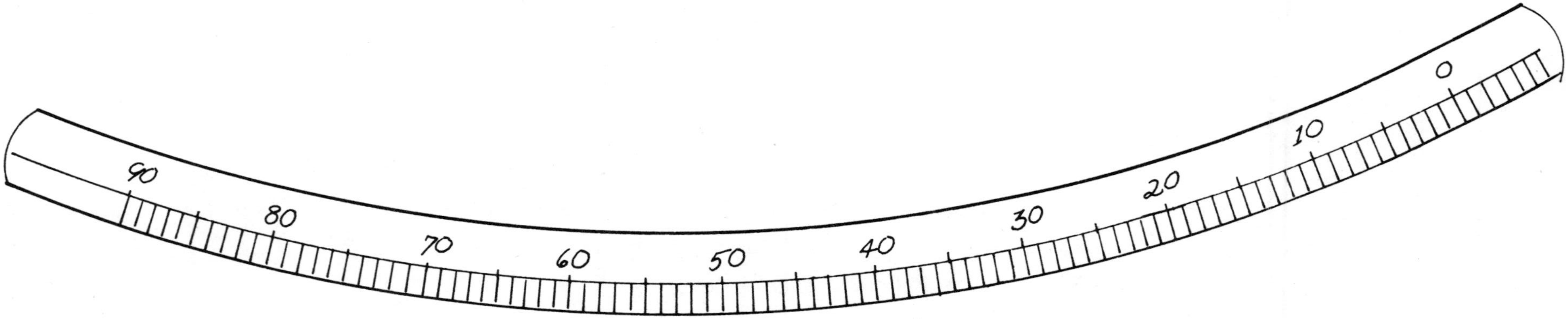

what remains of the ¼-inch ply and draw a 1-inch-diameter circle on it with a compass, making sure the circle just touches one edge. Then drill a ⅜-inch hole in the center of the circle and screw the wood to a piece of scrap so it turns without wobbling and overhangs the scrap slightly on one side

Clamp the scrap to the table of a scroll saw so the blade rests against the plywood's overhanging edge where the circle touches. Turn on the saw and carefully rotate the wood past the saw's blade. The result will be a perfect circle. Countersink its hole for a ⁵⁄₁₆-inch-diameter flat-head bolt. Keep this disk handy—you'll need it a little later.

The index arm attaches to the frame at a pivot hole ⅞-inch from the top center of the index arm and from the top center of the frame. Countersink the outer face of the index arm (the face with the bev-elled sill) to accept a 1-inch long, ⁵⁄₁₆-inch diameter flathead bolt.

Sand and finish these pieces any way you like. Plywood octants look good if the frame and index arm are painted gloss black to simu-late ebony. You can varnish the horizon mirror disk if you desire a glossy finish, but traditionally these instruments were rubbed with beeswax polish. Some instrument makers attached ivory figuring

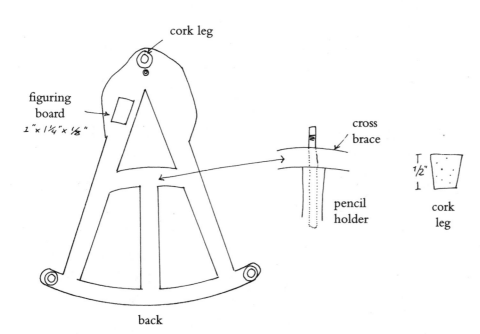

back

Figure 19-7
Optional extras: pencil holder, cork legs, and figur-ing board.

boards to their sextant frames. Calculations, time, and other notes could be penciled on these boards then erased after the data was entered in the log. A ⅛-inch-thick piece of plastic or ivory substitute can be fastened to the back of your frame with epoxy or ¼-inch brads.

Also, sextants often had pencil holders built into their braces. This is just a ³⁄₁₆-inch hole drilled through the top of the crosspiece about 5 inches into the brace. (This is not an option on one-piece frames.)

The maker and date, and sometimes the owner's name, were often engraved somewhere on the instrument. Hadley's instruments had a plaque in the center of the curving crosspiece. Humphrey Cole of London placed his name on the arc. One octant I saw had the maker's name by the horizon mirror.

To protect the instrument, and your brightwork, glue ½-inch cork "legs" to the corners of the frame on the side opposite the index arm.

You need to be as precise as possible in locating the arc scale and vernier, otherwise the accuracy of your instrument will be compromised. Using your patterns, draw register marks on the frame and arm to insure proper alignment of these scales. Also, fit the index arm temporarily to the frame with its ³⁄₁₆-inch flathead bolt, place a pencil inside the window and against the bevel, and swing the arm so the pencil draws an arc on the limb.

The bottom of the arc scale should line up exactly with this register mark so the vernier can be used. Now glue the arc scale to the limb and the vernier to the bevel in the index-arm window. Avoid getting any glue on the upper surfaces.

Finally, protect both scales with several coats of shellac. Lay on the coats carefully, sanding between each coat with very fine paper and rubbing with a tack cloth to pick up the fine dust

The Shade Glasses

The two shade glasses located between the index mirror and the horizon mirror reduce glare from the sun when taking sun sights and allow you to see clearly the reflected disk of the sun. They can be swung completely out of the way when taking star sights, or used singly, or in

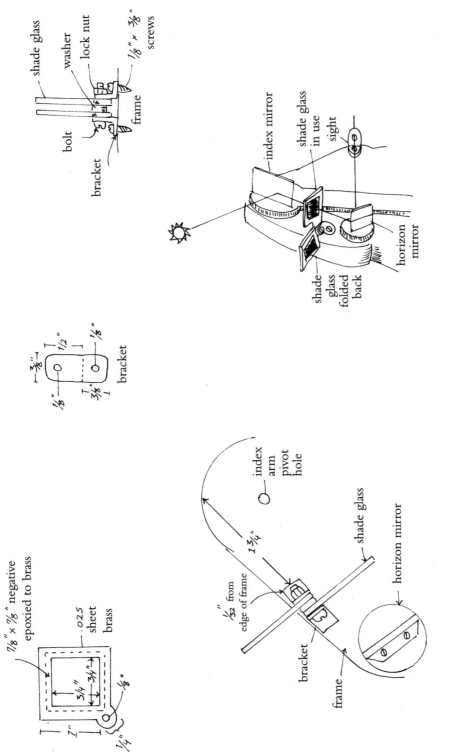

Figure 19-8
Details of the shade glasses.

shade glass

washer

lock nut

bolt

bracket

frame

1/8" × 3/8" screws

index mirror

shade glass in use

sight

horizon mirror

shade glass folded back

3/8"

1/2"

1/8"

1/8"

3/8"

bracket

7/8" × 7/8" negative epoxied to brass

.025 sheet brass

5/4"

3/4"

1/8"

1"

1"

1/4"

index arm pivot hole

1 3/4"

shade glass

horizon mirror

1/32" from edge of frame

bracket

frame

THE OCTANT 141

tandem, depending on the sun's intensity. The brackets and frames for the shade glasses are all made of .025-inch sheet brass cut with a coping saw. Follow the patterns in Figure 19-8. After the pieces are cut, lay the brackets on top of each other so their edges line up, clamp them together, and drill two ⅛-inch holes through both pieces. Bend them both into a right angle, then fasten the brackets to the sextant's frame with the roundhead brass screws and a dab of epoxy, as shown in Figure 19-8.

Each of the 1-inch × 1-inch brass frames on the shade glasses holds a piece of a completely exposed, developed, black-and-white negative. You can find these at the ends of developed rolls. Do not use negatives from color prints; they will not protect your eyes. Cut the darkest pieces into two ⅞-inch squares and epoxy them to the brass frames. Aluminized Mylar can also be used in place of negatives.

Put a ¼-inch diameter washer between the two frames to act as a spacer and attach the frames to the brackets with a ¼-inch bolt and locknut.

The Mirrors

When the octant was invented, clear, defect-free, optical glass was rare, so the first instruments had metal mirrors. These worked well enough, but tarnished rapidly and had to be polished often. As glass-making improved and sheets with optically flat faces became available, instrument makers replaced metal mirrors with glass mirrors. These first

Figure 19-9
Details of the mirrors.

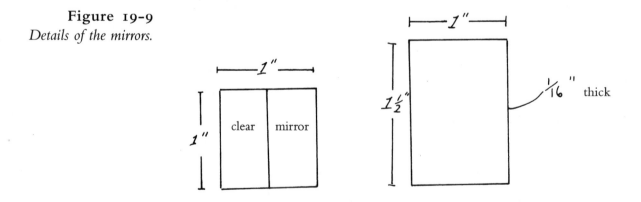

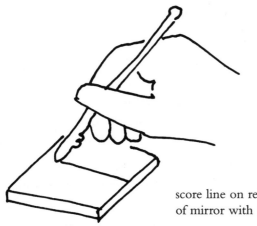

score line on reflective side
of mirror with glass cutter

tap reverse side to begin break

break in two along table edge

Figure 19-10
How to cut the mirror glass.

mirrors were quicksilvered. You can silver your own mirror, if you wish, following the instructions in *The Mirror Book* listed in the bibliography. Or you can buy a mirror ready-made. Either way, you'll need to cut your mirror into proper-sized pieces for the index mirror and horizon mirror.

It isn't difficult to cut glass successfully, especially along the straight lines these mirrors require. Start by scoring the glass with a cutter on the side opposite the film. Use unbroken strokes from one edge of the glass to the other. Then turn the glass over and give it a sharp tap or two to prepare the glass for breaking, but not hard enough to scratch the film. You can pad the cutter with a piece of tape for this step.

Turn the glass over again so the scored side is up, place the scored line along a straight edge such as a tabletop protected with cloth, and break the glass along the score. If the edges of the glass are too sharp, round them slightly with an oilstone.

Take the 1-inch × 1-inch horizon mirror and turn it over so the non-reflecting film side faces up. Mark one edge as the top and draw a pencil line perpendicular to the top edge that bisects the mirror. With a sharp, single-edged razor blade, carefully shave off all the mirror film on the right side of the horizon glass. Then gently rub off the remaining haze with a moist cloth dipped in rubbing compound or an abrasive cleaner like Comet. Don't rub too hard or you'll scratch the glass. When the right side is completely transparent, rinse it with tap water and let it dry.

The Sight and Clip

Cut the sight out of the .025-inch sheet brass with a coping saw fitted with a metal-cutting blade; finish the edges with a grinding wheel and file. Drill the sight hole and bend the sight as shown in Figure 19-11. For additional eye protection when sighting the sun, the sight on this sextant features a clip to hold small pieces of film. With a pair of scissors, cut the clip out of .005-inch sheet brass and bend it into shape with needle-nosed pliers or your fingers. Again, I use the exposed black-and-white negatives cut into ½-inch by ¾-inch pieces. You can

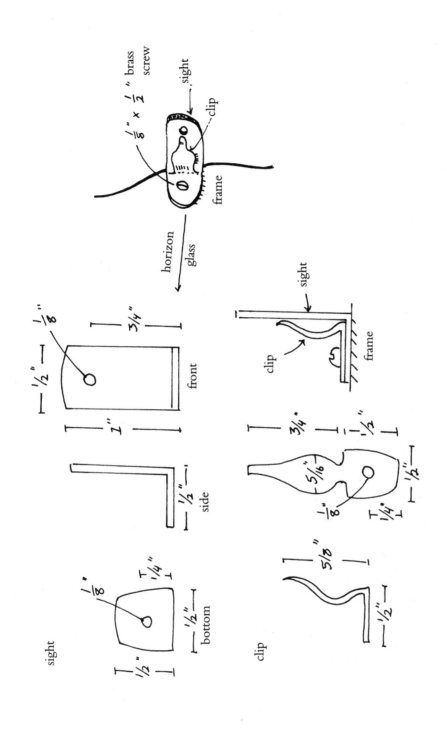

Figure 19-11
Details of the sight and the clip.

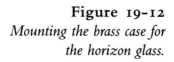

Figure 19-12
*Mounting the brass case for
the horizon glass.*

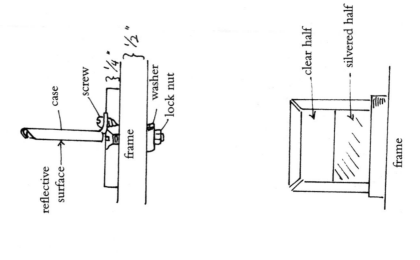

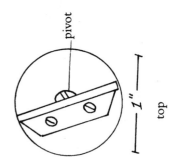

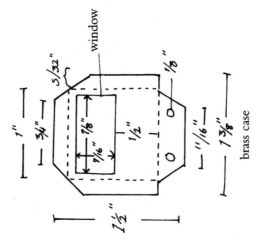

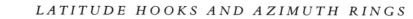

layer a couple of pieces between the pinnule and the clip to get the right combination of darkness and transparency. I store my pieces of film in a small plastic Ziploc bag taped to the back of the instrument.

Attach the sight and clip to the frame 2¼ inches from the index arm's pivot point using a ½-inch roundheadbrass screw and epoxy glue.

Assembling the Horizon Mirror

Now you can make and assemble the parts for horizon mirror. The mirror itself fits in a brass case mounted on the 1-inch diameter wooden disk you made earlier. This case protects the silvered side of the mirror and has a rectangular window through which the horizon is sighted.

Following the pattern in Figure 19-12, cut the case out of .025-inch sheet brass using a coping saw. To make the case's window, first drill a small hole in each corner, then cut between them with a coping saw. Finish the edges with a file, drill two ⅛-inch holes for the mount-

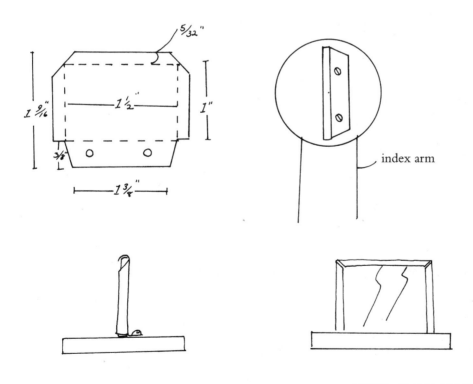

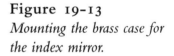
index arm

Figure 19-13
Mounting the brass case for the index mirror.

Figure 19-14
Aligning the index mirror.

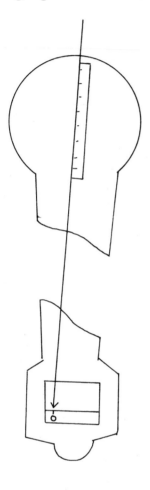

ing screws in the bottom flange, and bend the bottom flange perpendicular to the casing.

There's less risk of damaging the mirror if you first fit the case to a template the same size and thickness as the horizon mirror. I use a piece of Plexiglas. Bend the metal flaps around the template until it is snug but can still move. Remove the template and insert the mirror so the reflective film is against the brass and the clear portion fits in the window. Then gently tighten the flaps with pliers until the glass doesn't wobble.

Next, epoxy the head of a 1-inch flathead bolt to the disk's center hole. Make sure the head is flush with the disk and be careful to wipe off any drips that might squeeze out. After the epoxy cures, take the horizon mirror case and align the middle of its front face (the side with the mirror) over the center of the bolt. Fasten the case to the disk with two, ⁵⁄₁₆-inch roundhead screws dabbed in epoxy.

Finally, attach the disk to the frame with a washer and locknut. The locknut should be just tight enough to allow the disk to turn.

Assembling the Index Arm and Mirror

Now you can assemble the index arm. First, make a case for the index mirror following the same steps used for the horizon glass; drill two ¼-inch holes in the mounting flange. These are deliberately oversized. Then epoxy the head of a 1-inch flathead bolt flush to the hole at the top of the index arm and wipe away any drips before the epoxy cures.

The case is mounted on the index arm so the mirror's front face is in line with the center of the bolt and with 0 degrees on the vernier scale. Use two ⅜-inch-long roundhead screws and a dab of epoxy to fasten the case to the index arm, but don't tighten the screws all the way. Before the epoxy cures, lay a straightedge along the face of the mirror to double-check that it lines up with 0 on the vernier. The oversized holes in the case's mounting flange will allow you to move the case slightly before the epoxy cures.

When the mirror is properly positioned, snug up the screws. Perform this step with care. Any misalignment between the index mirror and the vernier will result in index error, which will have to be factored into all readings taken with your octant.

Now you can mount the index arm to the frame. First, place the thinnest brass washer you can find over the bolt. If there's nothing suitable, cut out a 1-inch square of .005-inch sheet brass and drill a ³⁄₁₆-inch hole in its center. Then insert the bolt into the top of the frame and fasten it with a washer and locknut. The arm should move easily but stay in position without falling back, even if the instrument is shaken.

Final Adjustments

Your octant is now ready for some fine-tuning:

Index mirror

Check first to see that the index mirror is absolutely perpendicular to the frame. To do this, hold the instrument horizontally with the arc pointed away from you and so you can see the arc reflected in the index mirror. The arc and its reflection should line up exactly, as shown in Figure 19-15. If not, tweak the case gently with a pair of pliers. If the reflection is lower than the real arc, the index mirror must be bent toward the horizon mirror. If the reflection is higher than the real arc, bend the index mirror away from the horizon mirror.

Next, you'll need to rotate the horizon mirror to its proper posi-

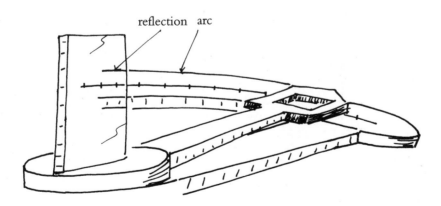

reflection arc

Figure 19-15
Checking the index mirror for perpendicularity.

Figure 19-16
Setting the mirror faces.

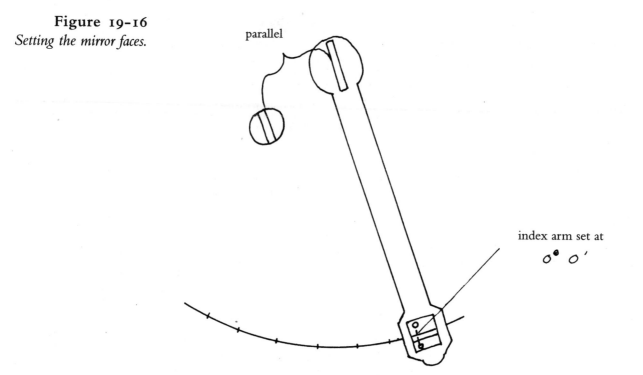

parallel

index arm set at

$0°\ 0'$

tion. Swing the index arm so that 0 on the vernier lines up with 0 on the arc scale (0 degrees, 0 minutes) and loosen the disk's locknut. As you hold the instrument vertically, sight the horizon through the pinnule and horizon glass, then rotate the disk until the reflected horizon and real horizon line up. Tighten the disk's locknut firmly. The horizon glass is now angled approximately 20 degrees from the centerline of the instrument.

Figure 19-17
Checking for side error.

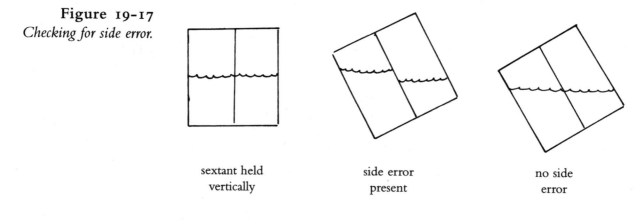

sextant held
vertically

side error
present

no side
error

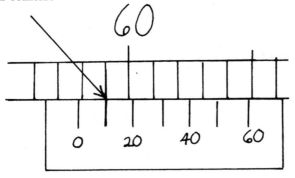

arc and vernier
marks coincide

sextant reads

62° 10′

Figure 19-18
*How to read the degree
scale and the vernier scale.*

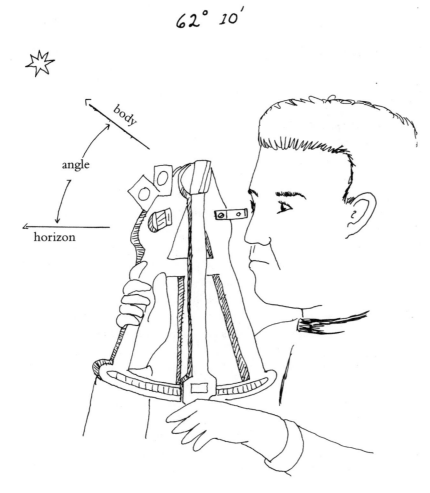

Figure 19-19
*Sighting a celestial body
with an octant.*

Side error

You also have to make sure the horizon glass is square to the frame. Once again, hold your octant vertically, sight the horizon, and move the index arm until the real and reflected horizons line up. Now tilt the instrument from side to side. If there's a break between the horizon and its reflected image while the instrument is tilted, the horizon glass is not perpendicular to the frame. To correct this side error, carefully adjust the glass with a pair of pliers until the break disappears for both right-hand and left-hand tilt. If the reflected horizon is below the real horizon when the instrument is tilted to the left, bend the horizon mirror case away from the sight. If the reflected image is above the real

---

Using Your Octant: A Noon Sight

A noon sight of the sun is just as simple as a Pole Star sight. You'll need to know when the sun will cross your meridian, of course, and the quickest way to find that out is to go to the almanac and inspect the column that gives the Sun's Greenwich Hour Angle (GHA).

If you're west of Greenwich, simply look down the column for the longitude closest to yours and note the time given. That's when the sun will be directly over your head. If you're east of Greenwich, subtract your longitude from 360 degrees, and look down the Sun's GHA column for that figure. That's your local noon. Don't forget that all times are Greenwich Mean Time (GMT).

The simplest way to take the sight is as follows. Put the shade glasses in position on your sextant and when it's about 10 minutes before noon, face the sun and sight your horizon through the clear part of the horizon mirror. You don't need an ocean's horizon; the far shore of a good-sized lake will do. Move the index arm away from you until the image of the sun appears on the horizon mirror, then carefully adjust the index arm so the sun's lower limb—its bottom edge—appears just to touch the horizon. As the sun's reflection continues its rise, a gap will open between the reflected image and the horizon. Continue moving the index arm away from you so the reflected sun remains in contact with the horizon. As the sun approaches maximum altitude, it will move more and more slowly until it seems to stop. Remove your hand from the index arm and wait. In a moment or so, the reflection will start to dip into the horizon, so you can be sure you caught the sun at its highest point. The arc scale now shows the observed altitude.

To get a true altitude from that sight, you have to apply the same cor-

horizon, bend the case toward the sight. When the instrument is tilted to the right, the reverse applies.

If you don't have a convenient horizon, you can correct side error by sighting on a star. Move the index arm back and forth so the star's reflection moves vertically up and down along the boundary between the horizon mirror's silvered and clear halves. If the reflection's track tilts off to one side or the other, or doesn't touch the clear half, then side error is present.

If the reflected image of the star is to the right of real star, bend the case toward the sight. If the reflection is to the left of the real star, bend the case away from the sight. Finally, you need to check your device for index error, the amount the instrument is off after all other

---

rections as you did for Polaris: index error, dip, refraction and—an additional one for the sun—semi-diameter.

The sun is about 32 minutes in diameter, and your calculations presume you shot the middle of the sun. In fact, however, it's usually more convenient to let the sun's lower limb touch the horizon—in which case, you must add 16 minutes to your observed altitude. If the bottom limb is obscured by cloud, and you shoot the top limb, you must subtract 16 minutes. With the highest altitude as your observed altitude, and the corrections applied to give you true altitude, you can work out your latitude with simple arithmetic. Let's presume you took a sight in August somewhere north of 50 degrees latitude. Here's how your workings would look:

90 00

-57 28 True altitude

32 32 Zenith distance

17 57 Declination N (Add when same name as Lat.)

50 29 Latitude

Note that zenith distance is simply the sun's altitude subtracted from 90 degrees. The sun's declination north or south of the equator is obtained from the nautical almanac for the GMT of your sight. When your latitude and the sun's declination are on the same side of the equator (same name) you add declination to the zenith distance. When they're on opposite sides (different names) you subtract the declination.

*A simple primer on celestial navigation, such as Mary Blewitt's **Celestial Navigation for Yachtsmen**, Second American Edition (International Marine, 1995), will help you get the most out of your octant.*

adjustments have been made. But to find index error—and use your octant—you have to know how to read the vernier.

Reading the vernier scale

Invented in the 1600s by the French soldier and mathematician Pierre Vernier, the vernier allows you to read much smaller divisions than you could possibly see or inscribe on an ordinary scale. The principle behind the vernier is simple: A vernier's graduations have a spacing slightly different from the graduations on a larger, companion scale. When the two scales are aligned next to each other, the vernier "magnifies" the reading. There are two types of verniers: forward-reading verniers, where the numbers run the same direction as the companion scale and with smaller divisions, and reverse-reading verniers where the numbers run opposite to the companion scale and have larger divisions.

Your octant uses a reverse vernier with graduations one-sixth larger than those on the arc. As a result, this vernier allows you to read angles to one-sixth of a degree, or tens of minutes. (There are 60 minutes in a degree.) While not as precise as the micrometer drums on modern sextants that read down to seconds, your vernier offers about as much precision as you can expect from this instrument. To read the scales, move the index arm until the object you are sighting is properly aligned with the horizon. The degree marking on the arc scale just to the right of 0 degrees on the vernier is the object's altitude in degrees. The marking on the vernier that most closely matches a degree mark on the arc gives you minutes. See Figure 19-18.

Index error

Now that you can read the vernier, you can check for index error. First, set the index arm at 0 degrees 0 minutes. Sight the horizon, and make sure the horizons still line up as perfectly as possible. (If not, loosen the locknut on the horizon-mirror disk, rotate the disk until the alignment is as close as you can get it, then retighten the locknut.)

Next, move the index arm until the two horizons line up perfectly. If the 0-minute mark on the vernier does not line up exactly with the 0-degree mark on the arc (it probably won't), you will have to apply an index correction to any sights you make with your octant. This is quite normal.

When 0 on the vernier lines up with a degree mark to the left of 0 on the arc, then it is said to be "on the arc." When 0 on the vernier lines up with a degree mark to the right of arc's 0, it is "off the arc." With this arc scale, you can be as much as 6 degrees off the arc. If the vernier's 0 falls between two degree readings on the arc, read the minutes off the vernier as described above. If the vernier's 0 is between two degree readings off the arc, read the vernier backwards. In other words, 0 becomes 60 minutes and 60 minutes becomes 0. Note carefully: Degree readings on the arc are subtracted from any subsequent sight. Degree readings off the arc are added to your calculations. If no horizon is handy, you can also find index error by sighting on a distant horizontal feature, such as a roofline, or on a star. Use the index arm to bring the reflected image of the roof or star exactly in line with the real roof or star. Once again, if 0 on the vernier is on the arc, subtract that degree reading from your sights. If 0 is off the arc, add the degree reading to your sights. That's it! Your octant is now ready for use.

Using Your Octant: An Artificial Horizon

Where you have no natural water-level horizon, you can find the sun's altitude with an artificial horizon. This can be any still body of water, a pan of used motor oil, or a specially manufactured artificial horizon such as that produced by the Davis Instruments Company listed in the index.

Lower the shade glasses, put the exposed film in the sight's clip to protect your eye from glare, and stand so you can see the sun's reflection in the water or oil. Sight on this reflection through the horizon mirror, then bring the reflected half of the sun down to the horizon mirror with the index arm so it matches the reflected half of the sun in the water. The reading on the arc scale will be exactly twice the sun's altitude, and you don't have to factor in dip or semidiameter corrections. However, because the arc scale only reads to 90 degrees, you can take sights this way only in the winter, when the sun is no more than 45 degrees above the horizon.

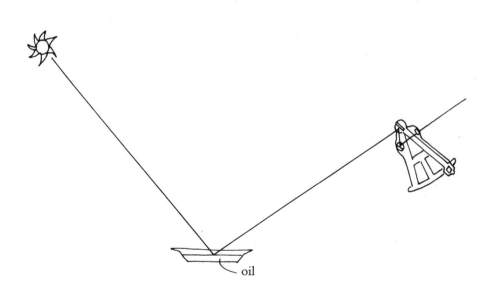

oil

Figure 19-20
Using an artificial horizon.

You can learn a lot about celestial navigation from this instrument. And though it isn't accurate enough to guide you through the coral reefs of tropical oceans, it will give you a reasonable idea of your position at sea, which could be a welcome check for the navigator. And it is fine for taking the vertical and horizontal sextant angles needed in coastal piloting. Be sure to recheck the mirrors periodically for perpendicularity, and side and index error.

As you will see, the octant—or sextant—is a versatile instrument and its usefulness increases with familiarity. The sextant I've shown you how to build is ideal for learning the fundamentals of celestial navigation and coastal piloting. And when the time comes to move on to a professionally made instrument, this sextant can go onto the bookcase as a conversation piece or into the ditch kit in case of emergencies. Anyone who spends time at sea should know how to use the sextant. In an age when we rely more and more on electronic devices to navigate for us, the sextant may seem mysterious, confusing, archaic. But it needn't be any of these things. Besides, it is far more rugged and reliable than any electronic instrument yet invented.

One of the best ways to take the mystery out of the sextant is to build one yourself and to use it often. Beyond all other devices, the sextant opens the sky and sea to your patient gaze. And it is a satisfying feeling to create a fine instrument with your own hands and have it work well.

Tools and Materials

Wm. Alvarez & Co.
135 South Bradford Ave.
Placentia, CA 92670
(Fastenings and fittings.)

Black Mountain Hardwoods
460 Riverside Dr.
Portland, ME 04901
(Tropical hardwoods.)

Boulter Plywood Corp.
Dept. WB
24 Broadway
Somerville, MA 02145
(Marine plywood, teak lumber
and veneer, mahogany.)

Edmund Scientific Co.
101 East Gloucester Pike
Barrington, NJ 08007
(Hard-to-find materials, equipment, instruments.)

Gougeon Brothers
P.O. Box X-908
Bay City, MI 48707
(Marine epoxies.)

Jamestown Distributors
P.O. Box 348
28 Narragansett Ave.
Jamestown, RI 02835
(Tools, fittings, fastenings.)

Model Expo
P.O. Box 1000
Mt. Pocono Park
Tobyhanna, PA 18466-1000
(Ship-model kits, modelers'
tools, wood, and metals.)

Niedermeyer, U.S.A.
P.O. Box 6737
Portland, OR 97228
(Wood and marine plywood.)

Wilcox-Crittenden
699 Middle St.
Middletown, CT 06457
(Bronze fittings and fastenings.)

Woodworkers Warehouse
For catalog, call: 1-800-366-6966
(Anything and everything in the
way of tools.)

Navigation Equipment

Celestaire
416 S. Pushing
Witchita, KS 67218
(Traditional celestial navigation equipment.)

Davis Instruments
3465 Diablo Ave.
Hayward, CA 94545-2746
(Plastic sextants, peloruses, artificial horizons, chart table instruments, etc. Write for catalog.)

Distribution Division, C44
National Ocean Survey
Riverdale, MD 20737
(Charts of U.S. waters. Write for free catalog.)

C. Plath N. America
222 Severn Ave.
Annapolis, MD 21403
(Weems and Plath piloting tools, sextants, etc.)

Recmar Marine
17875 Sky Park N.B.
Irvine, CA 92714
(Plotting tools.)

C Marine Catalogs

Crook & Crook
P.O. Box 190
2795 S.W. 27th Ave.
Miami, FL 33233

Defender Industries, Inc.
P.O. Box 820
255 Main St.
New Rochelle, NY 10820-0820

E & B Marine
210 Meadow Rd.
Edison, NJ 08818

Goldberg's Marine
P.O. Box 2597
330 Oregon Ave.
Philadelphia, PA 19147

Hamilton Marine, Inc.
P.O. Box 227
Searsport, ME 04974

**M & E Marine Supply
Company**
P.O. Box 601
Camden, NJ 08101

**Sailboat and Equipment
Directory**
SAIL magazine
275 Washington St.
Newton, MA 02158-1630

West Marine
(Attention Catalog)
P.O. Box 50050
Watsonville, CA 95077-5050

WoodenBoat Catalogs
P.O. Box 78
Naskeag Rd.
Brooklin, ME 04616

Bibliography

BAUER, Bruce. 1992. *The Sextant Handbook*, 2d ed. Camden, Me.: International Marine.

> The best, most accessible book I've found on the sextant, its use, and care. Read before buying a sextant.

BOURNE, William. 1963. *A Regiment for the Sea* (1574). London: The Hakluyt Society.

> An early English guide to navigation and the sea.

BREWINGTON, M. V. 1963. *The Peabody Museum Collection of Navigating Instruments*. Salem, Mass.

> An illustrated catalog of the museum's extensive holdings. Provides a wealth of detail on many early instruments and their makers.

BROWN, LLOYD A. 1949. *The Story of Maps*. New York: Dover Publications.

> Useful information on the development of early instruments.

CALLAHAN, Steven. 1986. *Adrift*. Boston: Houghton Mifflin Co.
>   In this gripping sea-adventure, Callahan explains his survival methods, including how to navigate with little more than pencils and rubber bands.

DEFENSE MAPPING AGENCY HYDROGRAPHIC CENTER. 1958. *American Practical Navigator*. Washington, D.C.
>   This classic, known to professional mariners as "Bowditch," covers everything from celestial navigation to lifeboat navigation, including useful information on using latitude hooks and cross-staffs as instruments of survival.

DODD, Edward. 1972. *Polynesian Seafaring*. New York: Dodd, Mead & Co.

GRAVES, Frederick. 1981. *Piloting*. Camden, Me.: International Marine.
>   The author makes piloting seem easy. A friendly book with useful sections on sextant and pelorus use.

KAUFMAN, Sidney. 1978. *Compass Adjusting for Small Craft*. Surfside, Fla.: Surfside Harbor Association.
>   In-depth advice on compass adjusting, setting up deviation tables, and using a sun compass and pelorus. Rare but worth tracking down.

LEWIS, Dr. David. 1972. *We, the Navigators*. Honolulu: University Press of Hawaii.
>   Lewis sailed with some of the last traditional Polynesian navigators and learned their secrets.

MALONEY, E. S. 1980. *Chapman's Piloting, Seamanship & Small Boat Handling*, 54th ed. New York: Hearst.
>   The complete resource on these topics.

MARKHAM, Albert H. 1880. *The Voyages and Works of John Davis.* London: The Hakluyt Society.
Contains *The Seaman's Secrets.*

MIXTER, George W. 1940. *Primer of Navigation.* Princeton: D. Van Nostrand & Co.
A good basic text.

MORISON, Samuel Eliot. 1942. *Admiral of the Ocean Sea: A Life of Christopher Columbus.* New York: Oxford University Press.
Admiral Morison sailed over Columbus's route. His book cleared up many misconceptions about the life and navigation techniques of the famous explorer.

MORISON, Samuel Eliot. 1971. *The European Discovery of America: the Northern Voyages.* New York: Oxford University Press.
Details the explorations and navigation methods of John Davis and others.

MORISON, Samuel Eliot. 1971. *The European Discovery of America: the Southern Voyages.* New York: Oxford University Press.
The story of early South-Atlantic crossings.

NAUTICAL ALMANAC. Annually. Washington, D.C.: U.S. Government Printing Office.

NEWMAN, J. Hartley and Lee Scott Newman. 1978. *The Mirror Book.* New York: Crown Publications.
Gives instructions for making silver mirrors.

RANDIER, Jean. 1980. *Marine Navigation Instruments.* London: John Murray.
Lavishly illustrated, this is an excellent resource for any instrument maker.

SCHLERETH, Hewitt. 1975. *Commonsense Celestial Navigation*. Chicago: Henry Regnery Co.

    Readable, easy-to-follow guide to basic celestial navigation.

TAYLOR, E. G. R. 1971. *The Haven-Finding Art*. London: Hollis and Carter.

    This fascinating history of navigation contains information on early instruments and navigation techniques.

VILLIERS, Alan J. 1940. *Sons of Sindbad*. New York: Charles Scribner's Sons.

    Seaman/author Villiers sailed on dhows in the late 1930s.

WAUGH, Albert E. 1973. *Sundials, Their Theory and Construction*. New York: Dover Publications.

Index